Rhetoric
and
the Founders

Rhetoric and the Founders

Dumas Malone,
Arthur Schlesinger, Jr., Norman Graebner, and Others

Volume 3
Exxon Education Foundation Series on Rhetoric and Political Discourse

Series Editor
Kenneth W. Thompson
White Burkett Miller Center of Public Affairs
University of Virginia

University Press of America

Lanham • New York • London

The Miller Center

University of Virginia

Library of Congress Cataloging-in-Publication Data

Malone, Dumas, 1892-
    Rhetoric and the founders.

    (Exxon Education Foundation series on rhetoric
and political discourse ; v. 3)
        1. Statesmen—United States—History—18th century—
Congresses. 2. United States—Politics and government—
1783-1809—Congresses. 3. Rhetoric—Political aspects—
United States—History—18th century—Congresses.
I. Schlesinger, Arthur Meier, 1917-   .
II. Graebner, Norman A. III. White Burkett Miller
Center. IV. Title. V. Series.
E302.5.M24 1987   973   87-14260
ISBN 0-8191-6465-8 (alk. paper)
ISBN 0-8191-6466-6 (pbk. : alk. paper)

The views expressed by the author(s) of this publication do not necessarily
represent the opinions of the Miller Center. We hold to Jefferson's dictum that:
"Truth is the proper and sufficient antagonist to error, and has nothing
to fear from the conflict, unless by human interposition, disarmed
of her natural weapons, free argument and debate."

Co-published by arrangement with
The White Burkett Miller Center of Public Affairs,
University of Virginia

All University Press of America books are produced on acid-free
paper which exceeds the minimum standards set by the National
Historical Publications and Records Commission.

Dedicated

to the

Memory

of

DUMAS MALONE

TABLE OF CONTENTS

PREFACE

From the time of its founding, the Miller Center benefited from the warmth and encouragement of historian Dumas Malone. The great Jeffersonian scholar attended the majority of Miller Center Forums. At these events, the custom of the Center was to turn to Mr. Malone to ask the final question of the speaker. By his very presence Mr. Malone has lent visible dignity and distinction to the Forums. Through his questions, he helped channel the participants' thinking toward more fundamental issues and problems. He deepened and enriched the intellectual life and programs of the Center.

In a series on rhetoric and political discourse in the United States, it would be inconceivable to omit the founding fathers. The United States stands alone among the nations of western civilization in achieving its golden age in political thought at the beginning of its history. Most nations of Europe achieved the full flowering of social and political thinking as they matured and developed. Historians ask themselves why the United States was a notable exception. What accounts for the richness of political and legal thought in The Federalist Papers? How could such a collection of remarkable men as Jefferson, Madison, Washington, John Adams, John Quincy Adams, James Monroe, Alexander Hamilton, Benjamin Franklin and John Jay all have been present at the founding? Why the contrast between this period and the later ones in American political thinking often without major intellectual and political figures? How could men of such unparalleled moral and political endowments appear suddenly and for a brief moment in American history in a country of a few million people? Why in recent times has no comparable group followed in their train?

In launching an inquiry into such questions, the rhetoric and political thought of the founders is properly the point of focus. What do we know about their approach to the style and content of political thought? What were

Preface

the personal and intellectual relationships of the leading
figures? How did each of them see his role and what
contributions did they make to one another's thought? Who
were the most creative forces and who the influences for
balance and proportion? What can be said about the
relations of Jefferson and Madison? Jefferson and Adams?
Jefferson and Hamilton?

It was questions such as these to which Mr. Malone
was addressing himself in Miller Center Forums before his
death. Other historian-participants included Norman A.
Graebner and Arthur Schlesinger, Jr., whose father, Arthur
Schlesinger, Sr., was Malone's close and longtime friend.
One of Mr. Malone's staunchest admirers among journalists
was Hugh Sidey who writes "The Presidency" column for
Time magazine. A brilliant young political scientist and
professor at Lynchburg College, Daniel G. Lang, is another
participant. Not surprisingly, the Center turned to this
group on Mr. Malone's death to complete the discussion he
had begun.

INTRODUCTION

If any body of political thought is timeless in American political thinking, it most assuredly is the political thought of the Founding Fathers. Whatever the topic or subject under discussion, contemporary Americans return to such classic works as *The Federalist.* Authority, power, the separation of powers and the presidency are themes that receive illumination in early American political writings. Rooted in the classics of western political thought and drawing on the wisdom of the Greeks and the Romans, the Founders bequeathed a legacy of political and rhetorical ideas that to this day remain unrivaled.

It is this body of thought that Mr. Malone was examining in a series of Forums at the Miller Center. Nearly blind and requiring a cane to assist his walking, he remained in full command of his thoughts to the end. As the text of his discussions makes clear, he spoke and responded with a kind of sovereign authority on minor details as well as broad issues concerning the Founders. Lesser state officials and their problems and accomplishments flashed across his mind. He demonstrated repeatedly an unfailing knowledge of men and events that participants found breathtaking. And he did all this with the zest and enthusiasm of a young man rather than a man in his mid-nineties. No one who heard and saw him at the Miller Center will forget him. Mr. Malone will remain forever a significant part of the Center's tradition.

Among his closest associates at the University was Norman A. Graebner, Randolph Compton Professor of Public Affairs at the Center. Their relationship was both personal and professional. Graebner and his friends took Mr. Malone to lunch every other week. When Graebner delivered the Commencement Address in the autumn of 1986, he chose to speak about the Founders. He was also the recipient in 1985 of the University's highest honor, the Thomas

Jefferson Award. In honoring the memory of Mr. Malone, Graebner has contributed a penetrating analysis of "Tradition, the Founding Fathers and Foreign Affairs." Quite possibly, the Miller Center's proudest accomplishment looking back from the 1990s will be the brilliant young scholars who are its intellectual heirs. A foremost figure in that group is Professor Daniel G. Lang, who is the author of *Foreign Policy in the Early Republic*. Lang and I have co-authored the paper "Human Rights and the Founding Fathers" but the chief merit of the work derives from Lang's original research on the Founders.

Mr. Malone felt very close to the two Schlesingers, Arthur, Sr. and Arthur, Jr., and when the younger Schlesinger spoke on the Kennedy Presidency at the Miller Center, Mr. Malone sat at his side. It is fitting that this little volume contain a paper by Professor Schlesinger on a topic he introduced in American political science literature, "The Imperial Presidency." Mr. Malone was troubled by developments in the American presidency, especially from 1981-86, and the theme Schlesinger addresses is therefore properly a part of this volume (I visited him in his last days and, in the aftermath of the Iran Contra disclosures, found him more distraught than I had ever seen him. He declared with passion: "Reagan will go down in history as one of our worst presidents.")

While Mr. Malone and Hugh Sidey often disagreed politely—one was liberal and the other had become more conservative in the Reagan era—they maintained a friendly relationship. Sidey participated in a lively Forum with Malone on "Jefferson and Madison." Sidey visited Malone whenever possible. They had planned another "Conversation at Monticello" which had to be postponed because of Malone's next to last illness. Sidey wrote an essay on Malone's *Jefferson* almost a decade ago which Malone always remembered. The enclosed essay is a much shorter piece which followed the Forum on "Jefferson and Madison."

With the publication of these Forums and papers, we seek to pay tribute to Mr. Malone. Yet no *festschrift*, however well intended, can do justice to his memory. For the University, he was perhaps the last remaining human linkage with Mr. Jefferson. To the Miller Center in its early history, he brought intellectual distinction, human warmth (who can forget the chuckle that accompanied his comments), historical sweep and perspective, and the relating of past with present and especially of Jefferson with the contemporary presidency. We shall not see his like again.

RHETORIC IN THE TIME OF JEFFERSON

Dumas Malone

NARRATOR: We thought it would be of great interest to inquire of you about discourse in the time of Jefferson, Hamilton, and Madison. We got into this whole area, Dumas, partly for very ignominious reasons. We were encouraged by the Exxon Education Foundation to have some discussions and prepare some publications on rhetoric and political discourse. Those were students of rhetoric who thought that at a presidential study center, there could well be useful consideration of the subject and we agreed. The moving spirit was the President of the Foundation.

The National Endowment for the Humanities about seven years ago had supported a program by three or four of the people who had been here to study rhetoric, but with a focus exclusively on presidential rhetoric as it manifested itself in the speech-making of Presidents. They invited one of President Nixon's speech writers and asked him what was the purpose of a speech, as he saw it, when he wrote speeches for President Nixon. He said "To kick the opposition in the stomach."

COMMENT: To put it politely!

NARRATOR: To put it politely. And we thought we would like to take a little broader view than that and go beyond the immediate political tactics and strategies.

In the fall we have had some lectures on the history and philosophy of rhetoric by some of the humanists on the faculty at the University of Virginia. David Grassmick, who is a graduate student, has been our graduate assistant collecting material and organizing information for this project.

We thought that it would be worthwhile to place the discussion in the context of what one might learn from the Founders. What was the role of political discourse in the time of the Founders? Who were engaged in the discourse? Was the setting and the environment utterly and totally different in that the mass media were not perhaps as prominent as they are today? Who discoursed with whom and to what end in the period of the Founders? These were some of the questions that we thought it would be useful to converse with you about. Maybe you'd just like to say a word in the beginning and then we can ask questions.

MR. MALONE: The first thing I ought to say is that anybody who can't see or hear any better than I can ought not to be participating in a colloquium. But I certainly don't want to do all the talking, and I'm afraid I'm not going to hear all that the rest of you are saying. I hope Kenneth will help me out in fielding questions and telling me what I am missing. And the other thing is that I not only don't hear everything, but I don't know who is speaking. I told Kenneth that this is a very interesting topic but it is sort of hard for me to define. I don't know really exactly what you are talking about.

There are some differences between the time of the Founders and this. It is perfectly obvious. They certainly didn't have TV, they didn't have radio, they didn't have a telephone, and they didn't have telegraph. They had none of those things. I would like to say it was as true of Jefferson as it was of Nebuchadnezzar that he never saw anything faster than a horse.

Another difference was in the use of the word rhetoric. The word rhetoric was not a bad word in that day. I did not take the precaution of looking it up in the NED (New English Dictionary) to see how the meaning of the word has changed through the years. The term rhetoric for me suggests a book I studied in my early teens, Lockwood and Emerson's *Composition and Rhetoric*. That's where I learned about the figures of speech—the difference between simile and metaphor, and the meaning of hyperbole.

I can't remember that Jefferson ever used the work rhetorical. He has a section on rhetoric in his catalog of his books. I didn't have a chance to look that up either

2

but I know exactly where it is. It wouldn't have been a derogatory term at any rate. But we think of rhetoric as being something that's shallow, and maybe even insincere. A good deal of communication was oral. I don't know if you want to get into the time of the American Revolution when the situation was so different from that of the early Republic. Most discourse had to be written because you couldn't reach as many people with speeches. There was no way to get an immense crowd together to hear a speech. I don't suppose there was really a big auditorium. The only way to get a thing circulated through the country would have to be by print, so the newspapers became terribly important because the newspapers were the media. Now we've got so many media.

Now what would you like me to talk about? I want to talk about Jefferson as a communicator. I think you might be interested in how Jefferson communicated. But I haven't prepared any speech. I thought maybe you'd ask me questions.

NARRATOR: Who'd like to ask the first question?

QUESTION: I'd really like to hear your views on Jefferson as a communicator: public speaking, writing, his ways of communicating, his style.

MR. MALONE: I could talk on that subject a long time. I don't know whether you want to include in that the Declaration of Independence.

COMMENT: I believe I've heard you say he was not a good public speaker.

MR. MALONE: He was not.

QUESTION: Does that mean he was a poor communicator?

MR. MALONE: No, he was not a good speaker. He was apparently all right up to a certain time but his voice would give out. It was reported that only half the people in the House of Representatives chamber could hear his two inaugural addresses. The acoustics were terrible, you may

3

be sure, and there was no microphone. That's another thing they didn't have. An orator had to have a lot of voice. Of course, that was true right on down to the time of William Jennings Bryan. One reason for Bryan's prominence and dominance in the convention in 1896 was his voice. Bryan could be heard in a vast assembly. Nowadays it doesn't make any difference whatever.

Well, let's go back to Jefferson. No, Jefferson was essentially a writer, not a speaker, and to a very remarkable degree his fame is dependent on the things he wrote. It was his writing from beginning to end that attracted public attention. He attracted attention in a committee because he was good at paperwork. That's how his career started out.

The most striking contrast between him and the present President is that he communicated so little. His communications to Congress were made in writing; he didn't deliver them in person. There were a lot of practical reasons for that. It was regarded as a very sensible decision because during the presidencies of Washington and Adams, when the government was in Philadelphia, Congress and the presidents were close together. The Congressional Committee had to reply to the President's address and they had only to go around the corner, so to speak, whereas in Washington they have to go the length of Pennsylvania Avenue, which was extremely inconvenient. Jefferson didn't want to deliver his message in person anyhow.

COMMENT: It was a good excuse.

MR. MALONE: Now when there is a great crisis in the country, the President goes on TV and makes a speech to the country explaining it. A great crisis of Jefferson's presidency was the Chesapeake affair. He didn't explain to his countrymen in any way what he was going to do. He didn't take any drastic action because he said that any government has a right to disavow the action of its agents, so the British government must be given that right. He had ordered the British ships out of the American harbors. They didn't go but he ordered them out. He did not explain to the country what he was doing in the way of negotiations. As a matter of fact, he kept diplomatic affairs pretty much to himself all the way through. An even more striking example is provided by the embargo. The embargo was a very important event, almost comparable to war. Economic warfare was adopted without any public explanation by the President. There was an explanation of it that came out in the *National Intelligence*, the paper in Washington. This was probably written by Madison though I am open to correction on that point. It was an unfortunate piece because it promised entirely too much for the embargo. Jefferson himself at no time made a public explanation of this very important issue. Historians have criticized him for not preparing the public for the sufferings that were involved.

I think the reason was partly because of his conception of the presidency, his conception of what the president should do. The separation of powers was almost a dogma at that time. The idea of separation of powers and a minimum of government was generally held. The exception was Hamilton and his crew. Jefferson took this principle of the separation of powers very seriously and he was not going to let the public think there was going to be tyranny. He didn't minimize the executive the way some of his colleagues did, nor did he want the legislature to dominate. He didn't want any group to dominate, and he was excessively careful not to appear to dictate in any way.

COMMENT: I think you are saying the embargo was unfortunate.

MR. MALONE: Yes. I didn't discuss the measure.

COMMENT: But let's take the piece of legislation the way he presented it. He was at the height of his power as President. That went to Congress and passed just like that. I think it took two or three days with no opposition whatever. The country didn't have time to talk about it. It went through Congress like the Gulf of Tonkin Resolution—the same kind of vote. It tore the country apart. The New Englanders were unanimously against it. They started smuggling, which shocked Jefferson. You can almost say that when a President is at the height of his

5

powers and the bill passes so easily, all hell is going to break loose whatever the result—whether it is the embargo, Gulf of Tonkin or whatever because it doesn't have enough discussion in the Congress. The President sees it go by so easily that he doesn't see what's ahead.

MR. MALONE: Well, I don't want to get too involved in that. It started out as a protective measure to save the American ships and shipping. As a matter of fact, in coming to Mr. Jefferson's rescue, you are quite right; there was practically no discussion, and it went quickly through Congress. It's important to note that there wasn't any power that he exercised under that law that wasn't given him by Congress. He did not assume any power. Lincoln, in the Civil War, assumed powers without being given them by Congress. Lincoln suspended the *habeas corpus* act without consent of Congress. The great powers exercised by Wilson and Roosevelt were given them by Congress. But we think Lincoln's action, given the circumstances, was warranted. I mean that is the general impression.

As I say, I don't want to get bogged down in the embargo. It went through a great many phases and was a terribly complicated thing—one of the toughest things anybody ever wants to tackle, at least historically. That's the worst thing I put Steve Hochman (Malone's research assistant) to doing. He said, "What are you going to do?" I said, "You get me the legislative history of the embargo." Most people who talk about it have no idea of its legislative history at all. They think it is one act; they just don't understand it.

My point is that Jefferson did not think of appealing to his countrymen as a whole in a way that presidents since then have. I doubt if there was any president that made much of that before Theodore Roosevelt. He is the one that talked about the presidency being a bully pulpit. Now you look them over. How many presidents can you think of who, as we now say, went over the heads of Congress to appeal to the people? Of course Lincoln made his great speech at Gettysburg and his wonderful second inaugural address, but these were formal occasions. Theodore Roosevelt is the first President that did it and he didn't make speeches so much with regard to particular acts of legislation as about general policies. The men who have appealed to the people with greatest success are Franklin Roosevelt and Ronald Reagan. They used radio and TV, and they couldn't conceivably have done so without them.

How, then, did Jefferson exercise his influence? This sounds contradictory, but actually Jefferson had enormous influence over Congress and he was enormously popular throughout the country. Most of the people in the country had never seen him. George Washington made presidential trips and so did James Monroe, but Jefferson never did.

He found out after a time that there had to be some leadership. And so he had a spokesman in Congress and that was the beginning of the majority leader. Jefferson was going to let other people do things for him; that was his procedure insofar as possible. He was an extraordinary executive in that respect. He worked through leaders. We think of him as a great popular leader, and of course he was, but he went through others and made practically no direct appeals to the people.

QUESTION: You emphasized that he was not a great public speaker and talked about the alternative ways in which he influenced people. Was he good in private or small group argumentation, face to face?

MR. MALONE: Oh, yes, he was very good, very convincing. He was very successful in getting people to do what he wanted them to do. Yes, he was very good. He was a good committeeman; when he was on committees he was a very effective member, but he didn't like public speaking. He was quite a private man in temperament.

I want to say one interesting thing about Jefferson and rhetoric. Jefferson used figures of speech a great deal; they came naturally to him. He used a great many nautical terms although he was not seagoing at all. He spoke of putting the ship on its Republican tack, you see. When he was trying to revise the Virginia Constitution, he said, "you can't expect a man to wear a coat that fit him when he was a boy." Things like that run all through Jefferson's writing. They are not conspicuous but you keep running into them.

The figure of speech that most interested him was the hyperbole. He was prone to exaggerate in private letters, not in public. I suppose you'd find some exaggeration in his public papers, but the notable examples of his hyperbole are in his private letters. The most extreme things that Jefferson ever said were always in letters, and nearly always addressed to the faithful. If he wanted to encourage someone who had written to him, he would cut loose. Some of the most often quoted passages of Jefferson are of that sort.

For example, the statement that "the tree of liberty has to be watered with the blood of tyrants and martyrs." That's true but it's a figure of speech, you see. And "I like a little rebellion now and then." People quote that to show he was a revolutionary type, which he was not. He was writing that to William S. Smith, who was the secretary to John Adams in London at the time of the Shays Rebellion. Nearly all the leaders in this country were excited about it. He was over in Europe and he said there was more violence in Europe, particularly in France, than in America.

What he wrote to William Short was the worst exaggeration. William Short was greatly disturbed by the people who were being killed in the French Revolution. He stayed on in France after Jefferson came back to this country. Jefferson wrote a letter to try to encourage him. He said on the whole more good than evil came from the Revolution, much as you might deplore these losses. And then he said "it would have been better if only Adam and Eve were left in every country than to be as we were." In other words, it would be better to have nobody but Adam and Eve left and to have everybody else destroyed and half of the world prostrated. Well, of course it was an utterly absurd remark. It is just a figure of speech, you see. He was very likely to use these figures of speech in writing to young men, like a teacher and his pupils. And I suppose there are some teachers who take a very pronounced opinion on something in order to stimulate their students.

QUESTION: When Jefferson said we must devoutly pray for Patrick Henry's death, was that a figure of speech or did he want Henry to die?

MR. MALONE: Well, I think he was probably glad to get rid of him. I didn't know he said that.

COMMENT: Yes. He wrote it to Madison. Madison said, "What are we going to do about Henry?" and Jefferson said, "Nothing, but we devoutly pray for his death."

MR. MALONE: Oh, well. Let's see about Patrick Henry. Most of what we know of Patrick Henry we get from Jefferson because Jefferson sent a great deal of material to William Wirt, who was writing the biography of Patrick Henry. Jefferson used a lot of this; he used everything that was favorable to Henry but he left out some that was unfavorable. But the editors of Jefferson's Papers rescued those so we can read them. History has really been greatly enriched by what Jefferson told us about Patrick Henry's services before the Revolution. He thought that Patrick Henry was the greatest orator that ever lived. Jefferson set a pretty high value on oratory as he thought the ancients did. Patrick Henry and Richard Henry Lee were referred to respectively as Demosthenes and Cicero—now that was regarded as a compliment, you see.

Wirt's book is absolutely fascinating. Wirt sent Jefferson the manuscript and Jefferson read it and sent it back with his comments. He said it was a little too flowery for his taste. One thing that Wirt had written was that Patrick Henry said he had read through a certain book twice. Jefferson said nobody who knew Henry could possibly believe he read any book twice. He doubted if he had ever read any book through. In other words, he had no opinion at all of Patrick Henry's learning. He thought his examination for the bar was quite a joke.

Anyway, Patrick Henry was actually the dominant figure in Virginia politics. He was not a bit intellectual. The issues of the American Revolution had been talked about in the House of Burgesses by a great many other people, but Henry had an ability to appeal to the emotions. Jefferson also said that Henry had a great understanding of the human heart. Jefferson wanted to give a balanced picture of him. He didn't have book learning but he understood people and was a very great orator.

9

COMMENT: But Jefferson never condemned that as rhetorical.

MR. MALONE: No, he didn't. He thought Patrick Henry was the first one to set the call of the Revolution in motion. He thought that was a good thing. But when it came to the problem of creating a government, Patrick Henry didn't have it. Jefferson and Madison regarded him as an obstructionist. They said that the constitution of Virginia was unsatisfactory but they didn't much want a convention to be called because Patrick Henry would dominate it and the Constitution might be worse than it had been before.

One thing that was very striking about that age was the use of the anonymous communication. I don't know when that ended, but as long as Jefferson lived it was still going on. Hamilton made use of anonymity in the controversy with Jefferson. I don't know how many of you are familiar with those anonymous communications but a great number of them are printed in the latest edition of Hamilton's writing. Even back in the days of Henry Cabot Lodge's edition a number of them were printed under various pseudonyms. There was a historian out in Ohio—I think his name was Marsh—who took great pleasure in finding additional anonymous pamphlets of contributions of Hamilton. He printed them in little pamphlets and kept sending them to me with glee.

Jefferson was secretary of state when Hamilton was secretary of the treasury. Hamilton wrote anonymous communications to the papers attacking Jefferson. There was one that was signed "Scourge" and that was the worst one. That was the most vulgar. I said, "Could it be possible that the man who wrote the opinion on the constitutionality of the Bank of the United States, which was a superb paper, also wrote this diatribe with all its vulgarity?" I wrote Marsh and said, "Are you sure of this? I don't want to make any mistake about it." He said, "Yes," and he gave me the reference to the Hamilton papers. The next time I was in Washington I looked it up and there it was. There was a great deal of that sort of thing. Papers were filled with communications signed by such names as

Hampton or Catullus or Scourge, and, of course, the famous *Federalist* papers came out anonymously.

COMMENT: Publius papers.

MR. MALONE: These communications were not all bad, but it may be that because of the anonymity they could be more abusive.

To go back to this business of Hamilton. Apparently what he did when he wrote "Scourge" or these other pamphlets was to fall into the style of writing of the political editors who were nearly all extremely partisan. That was a unique style of writing.

COMMENT: John Quincy Adams, commenting on this phenomenon, once said: "The public history of all countries is one thing, but the actual workings of the machinery must be foul." He preserved a high level of discourse on great issues of public policy.

MR. MALONE: Jefferson never wrote anonymous contributions to the papers. Madison did.

COMMENT: Jefferson egged him on.

QUESTION: Why don't you write something about this?

COMMENT: For God's sake, sir, take up your pen!!

MR. MALONE: Very late in Jefferson's life, when he was building the University of Virginia, he wrote a description of it, and he had it published anonymously.

COMMENT: All kinds of public political purposes are served by anonymity. Even today.

MR. MALONE: Today? Do we have anonymous publications in the good newspapers today?

COMMENT: "Official sources say that . . ." or "A high official says . . ."

11

MR. MALONE: Well, that would be in the news. Would any communications to the *Times* or the *Washington Post* ever be unsigned?

COMMENT: No.

COMMENT: The phenomenon that you are talking about ended, Dumas, when the great editors came on. When Greeley and those fellows came on the people knew who was in charge and the pseudonyms that you are talking about . . .

MR. MALONE: The political manners of the times were not good. They were very bad. There was a fight in the House of Representatives between Matthew Lyon of Vermont and Roger Griswold of Connecticut. I think Matthew Lyon is supposed to have spat in Griswold's face and Griswold is supposed to have hit him with a cane. Lyon is supposed to have defended himself with fire tongs. I can't think of any vituperation of any President since I have been keeping up with things which was as great as the vituperation of Jefferson's time.

The worst political campaign and the worst manners that I can remember was the election of 1928, the Al Smith-Herbert Hoover election. That was a dirty one. There was a great deal of evidence of a whispering campaign. The things they said about Mrs. Smith were perfectly horrid. That was a bad one.

It may be that there is vituperation comparable to that of Jefferson's time in publications that I don't see. There probably are publications in this country that would stop at nothing. That's perfectly possible. But so far as the good newspapers go, the manners are much better. Of course the congressmen and senators are shouting at each other a good deal, but they go to great pains to be polite to each other in public. They say, "As my distinguished friend, the senator from Montana says . . ." They go in for formality of that sort in a big way, much more than they did. I don't think they did that in the early days.

I have had the greatest admiration for the leaders in this early period. But politics was a pretty dirty game and everything was very partisan. It was black and white. The newspaper would know exactly what position it was going to take. Now of course you would find on occasion an attitude of independence as with Philip Freneau and William Duane. They were both men of very considerable independence. James Thompson Callender was the worst scandalmonger of the time.

Everything was partisan. Such and such a paper in Boston and such a paper in New York were Federalist papers, and such and such papers were Jeffersonian papers. I'd make a point in my research of getting something from each one. You wouldn't have to read them all because they all tended to say the same thing. They copied each other all the time.

COMMENT: A lot of these newspapers too were dependent for their revenue on public printing contracts from the state and federal governments. So they were full of patronage.

QUESTION: Did Jefferson feel called on to defend something like the Louisiana Purchase on a wider front than he would other matters? We hear so much about the excess of power of presidents today—the imperial presidency.

MR. MALONE: He was trying to avoid that. He never would have thought of himself as imperial. Everything about the Louisiana Purchase was affected by the requirements of speed. They had to go ahead. No, I don't think he did defend it publicly, but I can't remember.

QUESTION: To what extent did informal conversations between Madison, Monroe and Jefferson have any influence on the formation of policy?

MR. MALONE: The trouble is we don't know. There is political discourse at a high level in the correspondence of Jefferson and Madison. All the correspondence of Jefferson and Adams was more personal than the correspondence of Jefferson and Madison. They saw each other all the time and didn't need to get personal. The unfortunate thing about the relationship of Jefferson and Madison with regard to materials is that when they were together they didn't write each other. When Jefferson was in one place and Madison in another, they would keep each other informed. But when they were together they didn't do that in writing. Gallatin used to send little notes to Jefferson all the time. You can learn more from the correspondence of Gallatin and Jefferson during his presidency than from that of Jefferson and Madison. Some of the correspondence of Jefferson and Gallatin was extraordinarily illuminating. Jefferson wasn't going to stay in Washington in the sickly season so he'd always spend August and September at Monticello. Gallatin at about the same period was investigating the embargo in New York. His letters to Jefferson were very, very illuminating. In fact, I think I learned more about the enforcement problems of the embargo from those letters than from anything else.

I wish somebody would really do a study of the Jefferson-Madison correspondence.

COMMENT: Jim Smith is going to. He's got a grant.

MR. MALONE: Oh, that's fine because Adrianne Koch wrote a nice book which I learned a lot from. I think she helped but of course there is a lot more that could be done.

NARRATOR: Jim Young was talking a little bit yesterday about the extent to which the Founders commended their form of discourse. It's not quite what you were saying.

QUESTION: I was thinking out loud. It is not really much of a question. I was struck by the possibility that the form of leadership that got the country through the Revolution successfully, through the crisis of empire, and the kind of collective leadership that got the new nation a new constitution after the failure of the Articles of Confederation, did not provide the model of a proper government for the future that the Founders wrote into the Constitution where they sought to divide and share power, rather than to place anybody in charge or any one institution in charge. I was just sort of thinking out loud. I suppose that Jefferson was a central figure in the formation of a path of development for the United States. That is very contrary to the federalist vision of the teacher. And that was where his leadership as President was strongest, it seems to me.

MR. MALONE: You mean the division of powers was accentuated by Jefferson? That was not intended in the first inaugural address. It has the idea of a divided government, a limited government. People keep coming back to it for that reason.

I was reading the contemporary comments on the address, and nobody criticized it for the emphasis on a minimal government. The only person who did criticize it was Hamilton. His was almost the only voice of criticism that I could find; he criticized it for weeks after the first inaugural. Hamilton was, of course, an advocate of much greater centralization. John Adams was not in favor of centralization. He talked about checks and balances all the time. There is very little difference between him and Jefferson in their concepts of government except that he didn't have as much faith in people as Jefferson; he had a great deal more faith in the navy.

QUESTION: Jefferson was a consensus leader in that respect, wasn't he? He was very much more in tune with public sentiment on the role of government, the structure of government, and of territorial expansion rather than central economic development, strong navies and industry. He was very much more in the mood or aware of the public feeling, I would guess at that time, than Hamilton was. That's what you were saying. That was one reason perhaps why he could articulate that consensus and lead without the necessity all the time of making public declamation and public explanation.

MR. MALONE: That's a very good point.

QUESTION: Mr. Malone, you mentioned the Chesapeake incident and the embargo during Jefferson's time. I would ask you to comment upon the extent to which Jefferson's expression during his time influences British opinion toward the United States today.

The story that I'm going to tell you will be very brief. It occurred last week at a meeting of the English Speaking

Union, which was held in Farmington. The speaker of the evening was a man by the name of Mr. Burns who is director of the British Information Service in Washington in the British Embassy. His subject was diplomatic relations between England and the United States during the past two hundred years. His discourse lasted for almost an hour, at the conclusion of which the chairman asked if there were any questions from the audience. Being indiscreet as I am, I held up my hand and addressed the question as politely as I knew how, although there must have been some edge to it. I said that I had listened very attentively but I had missed two words during the speech: Thomas Jefferson. It was my understanding that Thomas Jefferson was the architect in part of the diplomatic relations between the United States and England about which this man was speaking. I wondered whether our host had mentioned to the guest that Thomas Jefferson was born here. Well, this created some disturbance among the audience and obviously modest discomfort for the speaker who embarrassingly replied he didn't know that and possibly he should have paid his respects.

The question period went in other directions but at the conclusion the chairman presented a memento of the occasion to Mr. Burns, the speaker. He said, "The developments of the evening have given me an opportunity to appropriately present to you six volumes of Dumas Malone on Thomas Jefferson."

MR. MALONE: Well, I'll tell you a story. The English Speaking Union was having a meeting here some years ago at which I had the honor to be the speaker. The British ambassador was present as a guest. I was speaking about the relations between Jefferson and the British. As a matter of fact Jefferson throughout most of his public life was quite anti-British. He was not, I think, pro-French but he was anti-British for reasons which were perfectly clear. Britain was the country that we had most to fear. I went through the reasons that Jefferson and the British really didn't get along; he thought the officials were terribly arrogant, as they were. I could see that some of my friends were becoming quite uneasy. I finally came to the time of the Monroe Doctrine when Jefferson wrote that letter to Monroe. It said, "When we have the British on our side we have nothing to fear, and we must of all things cultivate good relations with the British." So I knew all the time I had that up my sleeve to bring out.

The point is, he ceased to be anti-British when the reasons for his anti-British sentiment disappeared. They ceased to impress Americans into their naval service. They didn't announce that they were not going to impress them but after the Napoleonic wars they just stopped doing it. The British had been in a life and death struggle with the French and they didn't pay any attention to us. After the wars were all over, the situation was very good.

I think I would have been anti-British along with Mr. Jefferson in those early years, so I don't think he was wrong on that. I think the British were very much more at fault in the War of 1812 than we were, but I don't want to get into that. I don't think Jefferson was especially popular in England.

I was just thinking the other day that I can't remember ever seeing but one review of my books from England. That was of the first volumes and it was a very condescending review. It said: "I wonder why anybody would spend so much time on such a provincial figure."

What the English like most in American history is the Civil War. That's what they really love. I don't know what they think about Jefferson. You've been over lately, Bob. I suppose he just doesn't mean anything to them.

COMMENT: That's true. Libraries have very few American history books; they did have one of your six volumes.

MR. MALONE: One. That's just like them, you see.

COMMENT: You may be changing the attitude because when this man received your books with an embarrassed expression, he said, "Well, I'm certainly going to read them."

MR. MALONE: It's a very tangled story, of course. It's partly the result of a war. The British and the French were antagonistic the whole time, and we were caught in the cross fire. Of course we got hurt.

17

COMMENT: But Dumas, you remember that incident when Jefferson went over to visit Adams for a dinner party. Jefferson was seated next to a British general and this general said, "You know, when you want to come back into the empire, we're not going to take you; you are going to have to pay a price." He reported this to Madison and said, "That's the way people over there feel about us. You see they are arrogant, they think we are going to fail, and when we fail we're going to have to lick their boots to get back into the empire."

MR. MALONE: I think that's partly correct. I don't admire British officials of that period at all. Liberalism hadn't hit England yet. Later on, after the triumphs and the Napoleonic wars, they could afford to be liberal. But in this period they were not very likeable. I don't suppose any officials liked us, but the French at least were polite before the revolution. One thing about revolutionary governments; they are never polite. They just disregard the rules. But the French before the revolution were remarkably polite and Jefferson was very much taken by it.

QUESTION: Jefferson gave the British minister in Washington a bit of a hard time, didn't he?

MR. MALONE: He certainly did. Hamilton was consorting with the British minister in a way which I don't think would be tolerated today.

NARRATOR: May I ask one final question? Despite all these differences of the mass media and the different atmosphere, are there one or two lessons from this period that you think have meaning for the present? I was thinking about Jefferson's not feeling called on to make a speech after every issue. Is that a lesson? Is there a need for restraint based on his example?

MR. MALONE: I think so. Entirely apart from any analogy, I haven't really understood why there hasn't been a reaction already against Reagan's excessive communication. There will be. I'd be willing to bet that they will say it is too much.

One lesson to learn is that human nature has been pretty much the same, it seems to me, rather than having changed. I hate to say it is not improved. I think there are more civilized people than there used to be, but human nature still leaves a great deal to be desired. The tricks of the game are very similar, and I find that right through American history the same old tricks are used, such as name calling. That's a very ancient trick. They call the Jeffersonians Jacobins, just the same way McCarthy called so many people communists. Come to think about it, I don't think there is anybody in this period to be compared to McCarthy. I think McCarthy is the worst in American history. I can't think of anybody else that I would compare with McCarthy. But the tricks are the same. As a matter of fact, that is the case on both sides: Jefferson called his opponents monocrats. Well, there was more justification for that term than perhaps we think because after all there weren't many republics in the world at that time. Royalty was the rule not the exception. There may have been a real danger, but I think he exaggerated it. Anyway, he used the term monocrats; they used the term Jacobins, identifying them with the French Revolution just as later on communists were identified with Russia.

NARRATOR: We are terribly grateful to you. We wish we could do this every other week so that we'd be inspired and renewed in our thinking.

19

JEFFERSON AND MADISON

Dumas Malone

MR. THOMPSON: One time I had to introduce Reinhold Niebuhr on a panel and I said "This was like a bushleager introducing Mickey Mantle." It dates the story. But to introduce Dumas Malone and Hugh Sidey is much the same and they really need no introduction.

Dumas Malone was born in Coldwater, Mississippi. He is a graduate of Emory and his doctorate is from Yale. He taught at Harvard and was editor of the American Dictionary of Biography. He also was editor of Harvard University Press. He won the Pulitzer Prize for *Jefferson and His Time* and received numerous other awards. We are delighted that he chose at a crucial point in his career to come back to Virginia because he has contributed enormously.

This is the Miller Center's tenth anniversary and it is Hugh Sidey's twentieth anniversary as columnist on the American presidency at *Time* magazine. He is a graduate of Iowa State. He was born in Greenfield, Iowa and began as a reporter for a little paper, the *Adair County Free Press* before moving on to the *Omaha World Herald*. He came to *Life* magazine in 1955 and in 1956 to *Time*, and has interpreted the American presidency through these publishing outlets, and through a series of books, *John F. Kennedy, President; A Very Personal President* on Lyndon Baines Johnson; *Presidential Portrait* in 1975; *These United States*; and other writings that are well known. Both speakers have distinguished military service backgrounds.

We had planned a conversation some years ago at Monticello which had to be postponed. That's one reason for our discussion this morning. The other reason is that my most unforgettable intellectual experience in ten years at the University was hearing Dumas Malone talk about

Jefferson and Madison at a dinner organized by the Madison Papers Associates, as I remember. Everything about the meeting was unforgettable except one tragic omission. The discussion was never recorded. So partly to get a few of the ideas down in a form that many of us can read and read again and think about over time, partly to make up for a conversation that never occurred, we look forward to this morning's conversation on Jefferson and Madison and any related matters, including lessons for the present. Hugh Sidey will lead the discussion from here on.

MR. SIDEY: I'm really an interloper here; I'm kind of a traffic cop. I would hope that Dumas would carry the conversation. He's the expert. Just let me say that in thirty years of writing about the White House and the presidents who were there, it becomes increasingly clear to me that those who have a sense of history or some knowledge of it, no matter how they achieve it, are the better presidents in these moments of crisis that come along. And there is still a great need for those men, I think, who come from our political system to read more history and think about it, study it more. And I think maybe we are making a little progress. We now have Mr. Edmund Morris, the Pulitzer prize winning biographer of Theodore Roosevelt, who is in the White House cataloguing Mr. Reagan's last years. He will write a book when he's done. There is an awareness now that what goes before has shaped that institution. If some of the men in it have at least some knowledge of that, they are better presidents.

Well, let's hear from Dumas Malone and let's talk about that friendship between Madison and Jefferson. I wrote you before Christmas. You'll remember, I had been up in the private quarters of the White House. I had dinner with Mr. Reagan and I kept thinking of Dumas Malone all through dinner because he talked to me about the eye of Jefferson so many times, not only Jefferson's ideas about government but also his ideas about beauty and grace. That whole evening was special, it seemed to me, with the White House restored the way it was, and then when we went into the Oval Room and looked out over the South lawn at the Jefferson Memorial, it reminded me of Dumas. When I got home I wrote him a letter and said, "You know you were with us last night at that dinner."

About that friendship, was it extraordinary?

MR. MALONE: It certainly was. Perhaps I should say before we begin that I suppose this subject was chosen so it would be something that I could talk about.

MR. SIDEY: Journalists, whether they know it or not, can talk about anything. You know that.

MR. MALONE: Oh, yes. My friendship with you started years ago when you wrote a piece on Jefferson in *Time* which I liked and I wrote you a note to tell you that. And you came back at me and we've been going at it ever since. One thing you didn't mention about the Oval Room, is that the portrait of Jefferson was removed and replaced by one of Calvin Coolidge.

MR. SIDEY: Now we're into partisan politics. Leave that till later.

MR. MALONE: The friendship between Jefferson and Madison certainly was extraordinary. It has not attracted as much attention perhaps as the one between Jefferson and John Adams. Maybe one reason is that in the Jefferson and Adams relationship there was a breach and then there was a reconciliation. So there is a dramatic quality in it. There was no breach in the friendship between Jefferson and Madison in a matter of half a century. It is most extraordinary, certainly one of the most extraordinary friendships in American history.

There used to be a tendency to belittle Madison *vis-à-vis* Jefferson. I've never made the mistake of doing that. Madison was not even a disciple of Jefferson. You might say that Monroe was, but they started out as equals. There never was a time when Jefferson did not regard and treat Madison as a peer. That was equality. Nobody studying early American history can fail to gain an enormous respect for Madison. They had a common cultural background; they were both planters. They seemed to have started out by agreeing on practically everything. There was some

23

difference in their early experience which perhaps accounted for some difference in their very early relations. Jefferson was not in the United States during the time of the greatest turmoil which led to the Constitution. He was in France and he did not experience it directly. He tended to minimize it. He was comparing it all the time with the situation in Europe which, in turn, Madison had not seen. Jefferson was always making comparisons. He said "the Americans were so excited about Shays' Rebellion but there was more disorder in autocratic France than in democratic America." There was that difference between them and so at the outset Madison was probably more acutely aware of the need for a stronger government than Jefferson was. Jefferson was more aware of the ills of autocracy from seeing them in Europe.

There was the greatest tendency on the part of both the enemies and the admirers of Jefferson to overplay him in comparisons with Madison. The projection of the image of a man is a very striking thing and very often the image that goes around through the years is the one that is projected by his enemies. This was notoriously the case with Andrew Jackson, for example. The image which Jefferson's enemies set forth throughout his public career originated with Hamilton during their first conflict during Washington's administration. Hamilton wrote a series of anonymous pamphlets in which he attacked Jefferson and described him as an essentially ambitious, political driven man. That image has come on down through the years. It has only been dispelled in our own time. Hamilton was disposed to blame everything on Jefferson: whenever anything happened or whenever any criticism of his policy occurred he would say, "Oh, it went back to Jefferson, he was the fault of everything."

MR. SIDEY: We still do that.

MR. MALONE: That is still characteristic of procedure; we still tend to do precisely that, to overpersonalize issues. For example, in the days of the First World War everything was the Kaiser; in our days everything is the Russians; we often exaggerate.

Of course Hamilton had been very intimately associated with Madison in connection with the *Federalist Papers*. The first person of any prominence to criticize him publicly was not Jefferson, but Madison. If you want to pick out somebody who organized the first party of opposition, the person you've got to pick is Madison, not Jefferson. Yet both the enemies and friends have tended to give Jefferson exaggerated credit for it. But Madison started it. We talk about Jeffersonian democracy, or his term, republicanism. The republic is the great monarchy, and that caused some embarrassment in discussing the political situation because they always get confused with the present. But the party that we always think Jefferson founded and that came to be called Republican and then the Democratic party was really started by Madison. But Jefferson was a better symbol, somehow. The fact that Hamilton built him up—and Hamilton did have a great deal to do with it—made Jefferson the symbol. In other words, for Hamilton his criticism came back to him.

Then Jefferson's friends tend to do the same thing.

MR. SIDEY: Was there ever any friction between Madison and Jefferson?

MR. MALONE: Not to the outsider's view. They never let it be known. I'll have to ask the editor of the Madison Papers. At the moment I simply cannot think of any passage in Jefferson's writings that was critical of Madison. I can't think of one. Can you think of one, Bob?

MR. RUTLAND: No, it's the other way around, really. Rush asked Jefferson who the greatest man in the world was. Rush was hanging on his answer, and he said "James Madison," just like that. Of course he didn't elaborate but we all know what he meant. He admired his mind so much.

MR. MALONE: Well, I'm sure that's what he thought. Of course whenever they were together in the government they were thinking of the same thing. When I was dealing with Jefferson's last years under Madison's presidency, I was struck by the fact that there were some things that Madison did as President that Jefferson would not have done. For example, he would not have signed the charter of the Second Bank of the United States. Madison signed it. I don't think he ever thought it should have been done. But not one word of criticism of Madison from beginning to end. Jefferson gave Madison very little advice because he didn't want Madison to think that he was trying to tell him what to do. He was always trying to encourage him. On the other hand when Jefferson was President, he would submit his various public documents to the members of his Cabinet. I suppose he had submitted them to all members but Madison and Gallatin were the only ones that really counted. We have the record of their comments in many cases so we've got that criticism of Jefferson.

Jefferson had a good way of sending things around to Madison asking him what he thought about them. Now I don't know if Madison did that or not. I can't seem to remember that he did. When he was secretary of state he must have discussed his dispatches with Jefferson but they left no record in writing, at least I can't think of any. I've found enough of a disagreement between Jefferson and Madison's foreign policy to be worth noting. There was no particular difference. But Jefferson said things to Madison.

The letter in which Jefferson set forth the idea that the earth belongs always to the living generation is one that interests me a lot. Now if you are interested in looking that up, it is in a letter he wrote to Madison, on September 6, 1789, just before he left France. He didn't mail the letter until after he got back to America. I think Madison replied the next year. It is an extraordinarily interesting dialogue; but it is not easy reading at all, it is very tough reading. Anyway I had that letter read over to me the other day just as a matter of interest.

Jefferson had the idea that the earth always belongs to the living generation. He said "that's self evident, that's a self-evident truth." The dead don't have any rights, it is the living who do. You don't have to consider the dead, you have to think about the living. His particular application was in the financial area. He was in France and the French government was passing debts on to the next generation. Jefferson asked if they had a right to do it, and his position was that they didn't. He applied that to debts and he applied it also to laws and to constitutions.

He went into an elaborate discussion of what a generation consists of. This is very hard for me to follow and I need the help of a statistician, but he used the available mortality tables. He said that "no group of society is to pass on a debt beyond its own lifetime." And what is its lifetime? It's what the life time of the adults in a particular generation may expect of them. So he figured out it was 20 more years. He said that "all public debts should be on the basis of 20 years." That would be very interesting right now, wouldn't it?

MR. SIDEY: I'm very sorry; I think you've just given me a column to write.

MR. MALONE: Reagan could pick this up. I don't know why in the world he hasn't picked it up because it fits right in.

MR. SIDEY: Maybe because it's not on videotape.

MR. MALONE: I think it was hard for me to understand how he got the amount of 20 but it's 20 additional years, it isn't a particular time or session of the General Assembly of Virginia or the Congress of the United States. The adults on the average will live 20 more years; he figured that out on the basis of the statistical tables.

Now the other thing he applied it to was the constitutions and laws and he said that "they ought to be revised every 20 years." So debts were limited to 20 years, and public debt, of course, only to his presidency. He gave a large part of his efforts to trying to reduce the debt. He sent this to Madison and asked him what he thought of it. Madison's reply, which is a very interesting document, was, "Well, of course the interests of a President are paramount, that's obvious, but your applications are not realistic . . . There's a continuity in your own affairs and you can't define a generation with this arithmetical precision. It's not that clear-cut, it overlaps. One generation benefits from the actions of another. For example, in the American Revolution, we incurred a certain amount of debt but the American Revolution is beneficial to the present living generation." Jefferson accepted that; he would never argue on that point. Madison said with respect to the constitutional laws that "if you revise them every 20 years you are going to have complete confusion, it is not practical."

Well, there you are. That's a very good example. Here is Jefferson who discovered a great concept. Incidentally for Julian Boyd that is the only political idea that Jefferson picked up in his years abroad. He calls it "political relativism." It interests me enormously because it meant he recognized the inevitability of change. There is nobody in his generation, no statesman I know of who has the same conception of the inevitability of change. You are going to have change and you've got to adjust to it, you've got to adjust the institutions to it. The other side of the thing which I have made a great deal of is that every generation has to work out its own problems in the light of its own circumstances, and you're not doing it in the light of the times of Jefferson. If you wanted to determine the foreign policy of the United States, you don't get it out of Washington's Farewell Address. You've got to adjust that to the present needs. That's a great idea. It's a perfectly obvious idea.

But on the other hand you've got an idea of continuity. As far as I am concerned, too much change is wrong. Jefferson realized the necessity of change, and I'm only thinking about it now, with his relativistic view. He left himself the opportunity to change his own mind. That's one reason. There is no Jeffersonian school. There is no real body of Jeffersonian doctrine. Jeffersonianism is a way of looking at something.

It also serves to explain Jefferson's doctrine of strict construction of the Constitution. For a time I couldn't understand how a man of Jefferson's flexibility of mind would be so rigid. Well, he thought the Constitution should be changed every 20 years.

MR. SIDEY: He's got some support.

MR. MALONE: As far as I'm concerned there is a lack here. In this case too, he doesn't value tradition enough. I've always felt that way about Jefferson. He doesn't value tradition quite enough. Now whether Madison was much of a traditionalist, I don't know, but he was more realistic.

This is quite fascinating, but it is typical of Jefferson. He would have a great concept and he'd pursue it. He'd pursue it all the way. And Madison was more relativistic. There are a number of other cases.

MR. SIDEY: I would like to ask if history as you've watched over it these years changed the view of either of these men. Do you see change in their views?

MR. MALONE: Oh, yes, there was a change, and Jefferson could adjust himself. If he hadn't been able to adjust himself he would never have been successful. He had a ability to adjust himself to circumstances. But when it came to what he regarded as principle, he was awfully stubborn and very reluctant. Here is an example that illustrates the two men quite well.

In Jefferson's draft of the bill for establishing religious freedom, there are some sentences that were left out when the bill was passed, and they are sentences in which Jefferson emphasized intellectual independence compared to religious independence. For Jefferson, both were the same thing and he specifically stated something about intellectual freedom of the mind, which was supremely important to him. That bill went through when he was in France and Madison was the person who got it through. Madison consented to have these particular sentences deleted. That doesn't mean that Madison didn't believe in intellectual freedom; he did, I'm sure. And it doesn't mean that Jefferson might not have consented to the changes himself if he'd been here. I don't know. He might have, but that is a fact. But if he had not left those sentences out of the bill it might not have passed at all. Jefferson seemed to think that Madison was perfect; if Madison said a thing wouldn't do that ended it. He would accept it.

MR. SIDEY: Madison was in the government with Jefferson, but when he became President, Jefferson was a former President. How did he handle that?

MR. MALONE: He didn't intervene at all except to encourage him.

MR. SIDEY: He didn't criticize?

MR. MALONE: Oh, no, no indeed. He would never think of criticizing him.

MR. SIDEY: Was there communication back and forth?

MR. MALONE: Yes, all the time. There was only one trouble about the relations with Jefferson and Madison. In many cases they are not a matter of record because there is so much of it in conversation.

MR. SIDEY: Where did it start? Was it a family matter?

MR. MALONE: On, no, they met in the Virginia Assembly.

MR. SIDEY: That is after college?

MR. MALONE: When was it, Bob?

MR. RUTLAND: In 1778 or 1779, when Madison was on the Privy Council.

MR. MALONE: Yes, he was on the Council of State when Jefferson was governor.

MR. SIDEY: Was there any family relationship?

MR. MALONE: No, no family relationship.

MR. SIDEY: And this followed Princeton for Madison?

MR. RUTLAND: Quite a few years.

MR. THOMPSON: Dumas, you said one time that one of them was stronger as a speaker and in oral communications and that the other had a quality of precision in writing. Madison got the thing down in writing and was straightforward, whereas Jefferson articulated these ideas in speeches, letters and conversations.

MR. MALONE: Not in speeches but in letters. Madison was a much more cogent thinker than Jefferson; he was a more cogent thinker and a much better constitutional thinker, but his stuff is not as interesting to read. In his public papers—some of them of course are not as interesting as others—Jefferson has a natural tendency to use figures of speech. The first thing you notice is that you have a figure of speech almost always drawn out of nature. There it is, plopped right in the middle, and the result is that Jefferson is hardly ever dull. He is an extraordinarily interesting man whereas I've found some of Madison's papers pretty hard to get through. They are very cogent but they don't have this quality of imagination which Jefferson certainly had. There is almost something of a poetic quality that burst through. That also explains, in a way, one reason why Jefferson overshadowed Madison. Jefferson must have been more charismatic; actually, he must have been very charismatic. But he was not good with a crowd. He was not a good speaker. Madison was probably a better speaker than Jefferson, though neither one of them could be heard at a great distance. In those days they had no microphones which was an enormous disadvantage. The inaugural addresses of both of them was said to have been heard only by half of the people there.

But Madison was very effective in some of his speeches in the Congress. At the Virginia Ratifying Convention, for example, he was very effective indeed, more effective than Jefferson. But he could not have been as charismatic. He was a small man, but of course so was Hamilton. Hamilton was a small man and he was certainly a very dominant figure. I get the impression that Madison was a very likable man if you knew him.

MR. SIDEY: What rank did he have in the Cabinet during Jefferson's presidency? Was Madison Number One?

MR. MALONE: Oh, yes, number one. Louis Gallatin was the secretary of the treasury and those two were the men he consulted all the time. He said he had no secrets from

Madison. But Jefferson must have had a tremendous amount of personality.

QUESTION: We usually think of the cult of personality as a twentieth century phenomenon. Madison did not have a striking personality, whereas, even though Jefferson might not have been a good speaker, he did have a striking presence. He was a handsome person and had a towering presence. Would you comment on this aspect?

MR. MALONE: Yes, that's right. Yes, you are right, the personality emphasis was not as great as today. But everybody commented on it. Jefferson made an impression on everybody who met him. Of course everybody might not like him; some of them didn't like him at all. But he did have what we call presence; he had presence. He was not good-looking, but he was impressive. He was not like Washington. Washington, it was said, looked more like a king than George III, which really wasn't saying an awful lot. George III was a superb figure of a man and Jefferson was not quite that, but even so he was tall.

MR. SIDEY: What was his style as a President, Dumas, when he was in the White House? Did he use that presence a lot?

MR. MALONE: No, he dealt mostly with individuals. He had an enormous respect for progress and was very reluctant to let them know when he was telling them what to do. So he worked indirectly.

MR. SIDEY: He worked quietly.

MR. MALONE: I imagine Madison did too. I imagine they both worked the same way, but Jefferson had advantages that Madison did not have. After he got rid of Aaron Burr, Jefferson had no rivals in the party and Madison always had them. Jefferson had a prestige that always let him do things that Madison couldn't do. They both worked through persons; they didn't do things to the public at all. Jefferson didn't issue a public statement—he issued a proclamation or two. But as to such a thing as speaking in the time of crisis the way Reagan does, he never thought of it.

MR. SIDEY: Were most of the speeches to Congress?

MR. MALONE: He didn't make speeches, he didn't make speeches at all, except for the Indians. All the speeches he made were in normal addresses.

MR. SIDEY: And the rest were written messages.

MR. MALONE: He wrote messages. To the best of my knowledge he never made a political speech in his life.

MR. SIDEY: We should remember that his State of the Union message was sent up and read by a clerk.

MR. MALONE: Yes, probably drawn up by him. His Inaugural Address was also printed in advance and was made available for people.

MR. SIDEY: His conversation though, at his dining table, or in the White House at meetings, must have been quite remarkable.

MR. MALONE: Oh, yes, it certainly was. John Quincy Adams can attest to that. You know Adams couldn't help but express love and admiration for Jefferson. He scattered information; he didn't have wit like Franklin. I imagine Madison was supposed to be a good storyteller, but his conversation was probably in a way amusing. Is that right, Bob?

MR. RUTLAND: He was supposed to have been very good in small groups, and he even told some rather off-color stories.

MR. MALONE: It is said that "the most striking example of Madison's saving Jefferson from excess was in the case of the Kentucky-Virginia Resolution, and that's a terribly complicated subject which we really can't get into.

Incidentally, I think that of all the things I have had to work out with Jefferson, the Kentucky-Virginia

Resolution was the worst. That was the hardest. There was never a time that I was quite as dubious of Mr. Jefferson as in that period because that's the time he did some of what seemed to be his most reckless things.

Anyway, that was the time of the Alien and Sedition Acts and that certainly was one of the worst times in American history. The only time I ever met Mr. Truman, I congratulated his connection in the McCarthy era with the Alien and Sedition Acts. He saw the analogy right off. It was the same sort of hysterical period. It was probably the worst in our history. The fear in this case was the French Revolution, whereas in McCarthy's time it was the Russian Revolution. This was being employed for political purposes.

The Alien Act and, most importantly, the Sedition Act punished alleged libels on the government. What happened was that all branches of the government were apparently attempting to suppress freedom of speech. It was a hysterical time. The Supreme Court was utterly and completely partisan. It was a desperate time. The President, Congress and the Supreme Court were trying to destroy the political opposition. It was a desperate time and, therefore, excesses were perhaps to be expected.

This was all being done by the federal government. The Federalist party controlled all three branches of government and they were all going in for the suppression of freedom of speech and the destruction of their political opponents who they said were Jacobites, just as McCarthy said they were Communists. It is the same thing, it is all psychology. Since the federal government was united in support of these measures, how could Jefferson get at them? Well, the only way to do it was through the states. The states protested against the acts, especially against the Sedition Act.

Well, Jefferson's protests were expressed in the Kentucky Resolutions. It was not known until many years later that he wrote them. Of course he was vice president and if it were known that he wrote them, he might have been impeached. Madison wrote the Virginia Resolutions. The Kentucky Resolutions declared the Sedition Act unconstitutional and laid the foundation for states' rights doctrine. In his original draft, Jefferson said that the proper remedy to this is what we now call "nullification."

The word nullification was in his draft. The obviously unconstitutional aspect was that the state could nullify. Madison wouldn't stand for that and he did not see these resolutions. Jefferson drafted them and sent them to Wilson and Cary Nicholas who lived at Warren, down on the James River. John Breckenridge of Kentucky was visiting him and took them back to Kentucky. Jefferson had said he'd like Madison to see them, but Madison did not see them. If Madison had seen them the word nullification would have been struck out. As a matter of fact, it was struck out in Kentucky. It did not appear, even though we now know that Jefferson had it in there. We didn't know until fifteen or twenty years later that he wrote these.

Then Madison, who had started in Congress at this time, was elected to the Virginia Legislature and he presented the Virginia Resolutions which also were a protest against the Alien and Sedition Acts and took a state's rights position, but did not say anything about nullification. In other words, he was just protesting against them. This is a perfectly fascinating historical puzzle.

Then these resolutions were sent around to all the states and they got replies. The states didn't like them too well, especially the idea of nullification which was involved though it was not used. What was the reply? Well, Jefferson drafted a second Kentucky Resolution and in it he was firm about all he'd said before. He went so far as to virtually threaten secession. He made the point that the one thing that was worse than the disruption of the union was the complete dominance of the federal government or tyrannical government. That was not to be endured.

Madison found out about that and that word was left out of it. In the Virginia House of Delegates, Madison drew up the *Virginia Report* of 1800, which stated essentially the same theoretical position about the states and declared that the Sedition Act was unconstitutional. Yet it recognized that the position was a protest. It says so. That is a perfectly magnificent document and it could be described as the classic statement of the position of the party, particularly in Virginia at the time, but it was written by Madison, not by Jefferson. For Jefferson the Sedition Act was not only unconstitutional, but also it was null and void. He said that it was so bad and such an atrocious thing that no union was better than this. Jefferson felt that the Acts were null and void in themselves and couldn't be maintained. On his side, Madison didn't permit that and it was not in his draft. Jefferson accepted it and that was really the position of the party in Virginia for the next ten or fifteen years until John Taylor of Carolina came along, unfortunately.

Madison saved Jefferson from excess. After Jefferson's death, he said, "Allowance must be made for the habit in him as in others of great genius of expressing in strong and round terms the impression of the moral." Jefferson was likely to fly off the handle in times of intense excitement because he felt so strongly, and Madison was there to put on the brakes.

MR. SIDEY: You've previously mentioned, Dumas, the difference between the friendship of Madison and Jefferson and that of Adams and Jefferson. Have you anything to say on the difference between these relations?

MR. MALONE: Well, in certain respects I've sometimes said that Adams and Jefferson supplemented each other but not in quite the sense that Jefferson and Madison did. In the case of Jefferson and Madison it was a collaboration, which was immensely fruitful. In the case of Adams and Jefferson, it was not a collaboration. They actually were pretty much involved as you read about foreign policy but they didn't collaborate in bringing it about. Their discussion was late in their life, and it wasn't so much about the matters of the moment as it was about philosophical topics of one sort and another.

COMMENT: Of course you could take the Alien and Sedition Acts and explain them in terms of their reaction to the press. You remember the publication of those secrets by the Republican publishers in the Adams administration. It prosecuted them. Whereas, under the Jefferson administration some of those were prosecutions under different terms.

MR. MALONE: Well, that was during the period when they were at odds. Of course Adams was a very brilliant man and the attacks on him in the press were, as a matter of fact, no greater than those on Jefferson. And no worse than some on George Washington for that matter. But Adams was very vain and he couldn't take criticism. That was the grievance of Mrs. Adams. Abigail Adams had a fit when he pardoned some of the people like Gallatin who said so much about Adams.

MR. SIDEY: When they parted in public life, were they hostile to each other? Their later friendship of reconciliation was by letter, wasn't it?

MR. MALONE: Jefferson was elected President over Adams in 1801 and they didn't have anything to do with each other until 1812 when they were brought back together. The greatest difference between them was their view of human nature. Jefferson took a very favorable view of human nature, a little too favorable I think. Jefferson thought people were much more reasonable than they are likely to be. But it was wonderful that he did. I mean it was a wonderful thing that he did.

MR. SIDEY: Madison also had a pretty good view of human beings.

MR. MALONE: I imagine he did. I don't know so much about that. But Jefferson's view of people was essentially favorable and Adams grew up in the pessimistic tradition of New England.

MR. THOMPSON: Dumas, why did Madison and Jefferson or Jefferson and Adams trust one another in the face of all these differences? A whole succession of people have been here at the Miller Center and have spoken about postwar presidencies in the oral histories that we've done. In the Ford administration people, the Ford loyalists didn't trust the Nixon carry-overs and Ford didn't trust Reagan. In fact, when asked about the possibility of running with Reagan as a vice presidential candidate, his answer was, "I didn't understand him, I couldn't figure him out." Jefferson and Adams were two men with different points of view.

Why did they trust one another in the face of these differences?

MR. MALONE: Well, they had views with the same ends. The difference was the means, and, after all, they agreed far more than they disagreed. Of course Jefferson was a great conciliator in his party. He thought his function was to keep the party together, and he was not at all critical of other members of the party even though he didn't like them. He'd accept them.

I meant to say one thing. I could see what Jefferson got out of the relationship with Madison: by putting on the brakes on Jefferson, Madison saved him from recklessness. What did Madison get out of it? I can't prove this but I have an idea that Madison was at his best in Jefferson's company, that Jefferson drew out the best in Madison. They loved to talk and Jefferson was the catalyst. He was the mobilizer and he was a catalyst. Maybe that's the way we ought to think of Jefferson and his great influence in our history, as a catalyst.

MR. SIDEY: I'm just curious. Did he like Dolly Madison?

MR. MALONE: Oh, yes, oh, yes. Jefferson and Madison had an intimate relationship all the time. At Monticello one of the rooms was called "Mr. Madison's room." After all, they put Dolly's name in one of those places.

MR. SIDEY: Since we make so much fuss when we gather three contemporary ex-presidents—Nixon, Ford, and Carter—I noted that Madison, Jefferson and Monroe got together twice a year when they were out of office. What came out of those meetings?

MR. MALONE: They discussed things. Of course Madison and Monroe didn't get along too well all the time. Monroe was angered because he considered that he was ill-treated by the administration when he was minister to Great Britain and he tended to blame Madison for it. He was a rival of Madison for the nomination. He was put up by a few people. Jefferson didn't maintain quite the same intimacy with Monroe that he did with Madison. Of course he advised Monroe about the Monroe Doctrine, but he didn't think he had much influence with him.

MR. SIDEY: When I was on the phone with Dumas, I asked him to comment on contemporary affairs because I've been so fascinated watching what I would call the Jeffersonian doctrine of the rights of man being broadcast around the world and affecting the governments in Portugal, Spain, Argentina, Brazil, Haiti, and the Philippines. But of course that's a journalistic theory. You tell me if there is anything to that. It seems to me to live today through television all over the world.

MR. MALONE: That's good. I know you find this quite an encouraging thing.

MR. SIDEY: I do, yes.

MR. MALONE: I think they would. Jefferson was often very realistic and he was particularly realistic in the fields in which he knew most. When he was in France he was very much disturbed because he did not think the French people were ready to assume self-government. He said it was a great mistake that they ever got rid of the king. They ought to have kept him under a limited monarchy, and taken on democracy by degrees. They ought to try to be more like England at the time. They were not ready to have a self-government in the American sense. He said the same thing about the Spanish-American colonies when they revolted.

Now that doesn't mean he wouldn't be delighted with the overthrow of tyrants. Goodness knows, he spent most of his life seeking to overthrow tyranny. But this is the beginning. What worries me, and I'm sure worries you too, is what they are going to do in the Philippines. It could turn into an African country now.

You see, the difference between the American Revolution and almost all others was that the Americans already had a very high degree of self-government and they were trained in it. The Virginians were trained in it; they knew how to take over. So they just carried on and got rid of the king, the royal governor and royal officials, and things were pretty much the same. That's the reason he laid so much emphasis on education.

So I don't know what we can do for these people. God knows, I don't know what we can do for them. We ought to realize ourselves that these things are not accomplished quickly or easily. They are very difficult and very slow. It is going to take a long time.

MR. SIDEY: But the word has got to go out. I am absolutely convinced that this communications network is going to grow, and it is going to affect the Soviet Union. It already has in Eastern Europe.

MR. MALONE: You think it has already.

MR. SIDEY: Oh, yes. They cannot live beyond world opinion any more. It forces them out.

MR. MALONE: Of course that's what we always thought, that they eventually would be affected by it. I think they will.

MR. SIDEY: You see it now in Korea, and you see it in other places. You are right; they may not know what to do with it but they get the scent of freedom.

MR. MALONE: The State Department sent them a copy of my interview on Thomas Jefferson. I asked my son, "What will they do with that?" He said, "The reason they take it is not that they want it, they just want to keep up with what we are doing." They do that in their universities; they must have things that have been provided by the USIA, and they will probably affect them in time.

MR. SIDEY: One other question here. Recently, the historians did a big survey on the great Presidents. George Washington changed places with Franklin Roosevelt. The order was Lincoln, Franklin Roosevelt, Washington, and Jefferson. Does that please you? Does that make sense?

MR. MALONE: Well, I voted on all those things. I think they generally came out about the way I voted. I noticed that Jefferson has come up. Of course, they say just vote on the Presidents, nothing else. It is practically impossible to do that, you know. You can't help thinking about other things. For example, with Madison, you can't help thinking about what he did for the Constitution; it is almost impossible not to do it. I'd probably vote for him rather high on my list as a President. I always vote for Washington.

MR. SIDEY: He lost first place this last time.

MR. MALONE: Of course both Jefferson and Madison together with Washington, would have been great men even if they had never been President. In contrast, Lincoln and Roosevelt would not.

MR. SIDEY: Jefferson, Madison and Washington were on their own.

MR. THOMPSON: We made a promise to Dumas that we wouldn't try to make his presentation fit the fifty minute lecture that he used to give. We made a firm promise we'd limit the overall conversation to an hour. One reason for stopping, in addition to feeling that *pacta sunt servanda*, that treaties ought to be observed, is that we want to have him back. His so-called last hurrah is a myth and each time the discussion with him is better.

MR. MALONE: I'm sorry it was so much of a monologue. I told you you don't want to turn me loose. But I'm sorry that my friends here didn't have a real chance to question me. They will, though. The next time.

MR. THOMPSON: We thank both speakers today. Jefferson came only once in his country's history, Dumas Malone comes only once. It is unlikely that any historian will take his place.

HUMAN RIGHTS AND
THE FOUNDING FATHERS

Kenneth W. Thompson
and Daniel G. Lang

Few would dispute that the United States since "the creation" has displayed a concern for human rights. It is inconceivable that any observer could argue that a nation conceived in liberty and dedicated to the proposition that all men are created equal would not have recognized individual rights. Yet not only was the term "human rights" less often used by the founders but the classic texts of international law and politics in the eighteenth and nineteenth centuries subordinated it to other concepts.

Moreover, we dimly sense that the context in which human rights are discussed today has undergone a dramatic transformation. Whereas the setting for the discussion of rights once reflected emphasis on domestic aspirations, the last two administrations have adopted a crusading and ideological approach. It has been said that Lenin and Woodrow Wilson are the intellectual antipodes of the twentieth century. Each is a spokesman for a particular political religion. Marxism-Leninism has provided the Soviet Union with an ideology carrying worldwide appeal. The West has found its equivalent in a crusading human rights viewpoint. Human rights gives the United States something to stand for in the world; in the aftermath of Watergate it helped Americans to feel good about themselves again and to regain a sense of national self-respect. At the same time it marks a recrudescence of Wilsonianism.

More important, a human rights crusade means the global extension of American domestic politics. Human rights appeals enable Americans to link the values of our domestic life and the purposes of our foreign policy. They are also a domestically acceptable statement of the quest for a new world order. What is often left unsaid is that a world of universal human rights accepted by all peoples would be one in which national sovereignty would have been overcome. To define the human rights campaign as a long advance toward the ending of sovereignty would weaken the support of human rights by national public opinion. Thus, putting the stress on human rights helps mobilize domestic constituencies who favor global reform but would hesitate to support a new world order.

The Carter administration singled out human rights as the focal point of its crusade. The Reagan administration has moved in the direction of Project Democracy, a worldwide movement for extending democracy to peoples everywhere. Whereas some advisers in the Carter administration favored a new world order transcending sovereignty and national interest, Reagan policy-makers would maintain the state system but seek to help other nation states form democratic political orders or at least begin to achieve certain limited features of democratic rule. In both administrations the means to be used for the accomplish-ment of the worldwide mission were crusades, rather than the power of the example of human rights honored or of democracy working in one country.

It is the presence of the phenomenon of the crusading mission which characterizes the mid-twentieth century approach to human rights. The aim is to translate directly and immediately the American domestic into the international experience. In looking back to the approach of the American Founding Fathers, one finds a different approach and different emphases. First, the twentieth century version gives less attention to definition and rational formulation. It is often difficult to be sure what contemporary defenders of human rights intend. Do they mean to speak only of political and civil rights as human rights or do they consider social and economic rights equally valid? In considering violations of human rights do they identify such rights narrowly with personal security or broadly with rights to housing or employment?

Second, human rights can be judged in terms of the inspiring example of, say, a Universal Declaration of Human

Rights—a global abstraction and not a treaty with sanctions—or in terms of the consequences of human rights policy as practice. Accountability for human rights proclamations is harder to pin down than accountability for specific and narrowly defined policy. This leads to the question of how to make human rights the object of foreign policy. A more intelligent approach more consonant with experience is one that weighs human rights objectives against other objectives of foreign policy: for example, reducing international tensions or promoting arms control.

In other words, what critics say is called for is a discriminating rather than an indiscriminate human rights policy. If this requirement is important in the pursuit of human rights, then a return to the Founders' thought is clearly in order because they made such discriminating judgments and perhaps can teach us to do the same. A review of their approach reveals that they engaged in a process of moral reasoning in which they balanced competing goals and objectives and stressed consequences over intentions.

Participants in the debate about human rights and American foreign policy frequently refer to the American Founders and to the founding documents of the American policy—the Declaration of Independence and the Constitution. Less often do they explore what the leaders of that period meant by human rights and rarely do they consider the question of human rights with respect to the prevailing understanding of "the law of nature and nations," or the natural public law described by Hugo Grotius, Samuel Puffendorf, and, especially, Emmerich de Vattel. It is the effect of this body of thought on the Founders on which this paper will focus.[1] We will argue that "the law of nature and nations" discouraged states from making human rights the direct focus of foreign policy, but that it was nevertheless hopeful that human rights would be promoted indirectly, chiefly because of the operation of the balance of power system.

To understand how those who established the American republic approached the problem of human rights, it is helpful to consider three questions. First, what did they mean by human rights; second, what means did they propose to secure those rights; and third, how did they hope to promote human rights abroad? The paper will be divided accordingly. Particular attention will be paid to the writings of Alexander Hamilton and Thomas Jefferson, who played leading roles in the debate over the propriety of the American Revolution, yet who found themselves on opposite sides during the highly charged debates over foreign policy during the 1790s.

Definition of human rights

In the wake of the wars of the French Revolution and the rise of Napoleon, some interpreters of the American Revolution sought to downplay the importance of doctrines of human or "natural" rights in that Revolution. (While the Founders occasionally referred to "human rights," they more often talked about "the natural rights of mankind" and "inalienable" rights.) Friedrich von Gentz in his comparison of the American and the French revolutions, argued that the two were essentially different. Whereas the French Revolution was an offensive revolution which claimed the "rights of man" as its authority, the American Revolution was a defensive revolution which sought merely to preserve the rights owed Americans as Englishmen without advancing anything new or in conformity with "abstract ideas."[2] In fact, however, as John Adams later recalled, as the crisis with Great Britain intensified in 1774, American leaders discussed "whether We should recur to the Law of Nature, as well as to the British Constitution and our American Charters. Mr. Galloway and Mr. Duane were for excluding the Law of Nature. I was very strenuous for retaining and insisting on it."[3]

A cursory review of the writings of men such as Alexander Hamilton, Thomas Jefferson and others suggests that many joined Adams in resorting to "abstract" human rights as an important justification for the American Revolution, contrary to von Gentz. Alexander Hamilton argued in "A Full Vindication" that Parliament could have no rightful jurisdiction over the American colonies because the colonists had not given their consent to Parliament and such consent was the basis of natural justice.[4] He would later argue against the return of slaves freed by British troops to

46

their Southern masters on similar grounds. It had been wrong of the British to seduce away the slaves from their masters, but it would be even worse to return them to slavery when they had been promised and given their freedom: "the surrender of persons to slavery is an odious thing speaking in the language of the law of nations."[5]

Thomas Jefferson in his "Summary View of the Rights of British North America" grounded the American colonists' title to their colonies in the natural right "of departing from the country in which chance, not choice has placed them, of going in quest of new habitations, and of there establishing new societies."[6] In Jefferson's most famous formulation, governments which are instituted among men to secure the inalienable rights of life, liberty, and the pursuit of happiness derive "their just powers from the consent of the governed."

The first thing to be noticed about these references is that the Americans did not set natural against positve rights, but saw the two as complementary. Gentz himself pointed to this when he remarked that "never, in the whole course of the American revolution, were the rights of man appealed to for the destruction of the rights of a citizen."[7] The American revolutionists claimed their rights as Englishmen rested ultimately on their rights as human beings. Hamilton, for example, in his exchange with Samuel Seabury, argued that the Americans ought to be considered free of Parliament's jurisdiction because of natural justice, the fundamentals of the English constitution, *and* the particular grants in each colony's charter from the king.[8]

Another influential leader, James Wilson of Pennsylvania, similarly argued "that the principles on which we have founded our opposition to the late acts of Parliament are the principles of justice and freedom, and of the British Constitution."[9]

The second thing to notice is the effort made by the Americans to dissociate their account of the state of nature and natural rights from the account given by Hobbes. Notorious as an atheist and as a monarchical absolutist, Hobbes had also suggested that men had come together in society simply out of a sense of self-preservation and that all law was simply conventional. By contrast, the Founders' preferred authorities adhered to a milder view of human nature and suggested that there was a natural law which bound men even in the state of nature. When Seabury asked what Hamilton meant by "natural rights," Hamilton advised him to study the law of nature and commended to him the writings of Grotius, Puffendorf, Locke, Montesquieu, and Burlamaqui. Contrary to Hobbes, Hamilton wrote, good and wise men in all ages

> have supposed that the deity, from the relations we stand in to himself and to each other, has constituted an eternal and immutable law, which is, indispensably, obligatory upon all mankind, prior to any human institution whatever. . . . He endowed him with rational faculties by the help of which to discern and pursue such things as were consistent with his duty and his interest, and invested him with an inviolable right to personal liberty and to personal safety.[10]

It was this law of nature which the natural public law writers like Puffendorf and Vattel identified as the "necessary" law of nations, which is to say binding on all nations.

Third, it is important to point out that while these formulations resembled traditional natural law arguments, they depended much more heavily on the bedrock of the human desires for life, liberty and property. With modern political theory the moral horizon was lowered to include essentially what human beings were thought to want—independent of moral considerations.

Securing human rights

According to the new natural rights principles, civil government was established to secure the natural rights to life, liberty, and property, the enjoyment of which the "inconveniences" of the state of nature did not always permit. The question still remained, however, which form of civil government could best secure those rights? The Americans would provide a novel response.

Traditionally, political theorists and writers had held that the best form of government for securing human rights was republican government. Unfortunately, as Hamilton pointed out, "every man who speaks or writes on the subject has an arbitrary standard in his own mind."[11] Thus Rome, Sparta, Carthage, the Netherlands, Poland, and Great Britain had all been called republics notwithstanding strong monarchical and aristocratic elements. Indeed what made these polities identifiable as republics was their correspondence to the traditional ideal of mixed or balanced government in which was joined an aristocratic, a monarchical, and a democratic element. Burlamaqui, for example, wrote that the best forms of government "are either a limited monarchy or an aristocracy tempered with democracy by some privileges in favour of the body of the people."[12]

Tradition also had it that republics could only succeed when kept small; the larger a polity, the more necessary monarchical forms would be. Since most countries exceeded the optimal size for republican government, the best that could be hoped for human rights in their cases was some form of limited monarchy. To quote Burlamaqui again: "Great states can hardly admit of republican government; hence a monarchy, wisely limited, suits them better."[13]

The Americans overturned these traditional notions of republican government in at least two important respects, and in so doing generated new hope for the possibility of establishing republican government everywhere. First, the Americans established their republic on wholly democratic foundations and not on the basis of different social orders. The United States government, explained James Wilson, "is purely democratical: but that principle is applied in different forms, in order to obtain the advantages, and exclude the inconveniences of the simple modes of government."[14] By creating separate executive, legislative, and judicial institutions, by providing each branch with the means to check and balance each other, by dividing the legislature itself into two parts, and by incorporating the principle of representation into the government, the American Constitution provided "powerful means by which the excellencies of republican government may be retained and its imperfections lessened or avoided."[15]

Second, the Americans who identified themselves as Federalists in the debate over the merits of the proposed Constitution and who carried the day argued that human rights in republican government would be made more secure by enlarging its sphere. The problem with the small republics favored by traditional political science, Madison argued in Federalist 10, was the problem of majority tyranny. This could be avoided by encouraging diversity and diversity came with larger territory and population.

> Extend the sphere and you take in a greater variety of parties and interests; you make it less probable that a majority of the whole will have a common motive to invade the rights of other citizens; or if such a common motive exists, it will be more difficult for all who feel it to discover their own strength and to act in unison with each other.[16]

In short, if the Americans were right that republican government did not have to be built upon certain pre-existing social orders or within certain restrictive geographical limits, then there was reason to believe that the American Constitution could "present a model of Government for all the civilized nations of the earth."[17]

Promoting human rights

This new hope for republican government and the universalistic grounding of human rights in "the laws of Nature and Nature's God" encouraged a universalistic cast to American thinking about foreign policy. The law of nature itself seemed to support this: Vattel suggested that the first law of nature was a duty to help others. It was this duty which helped to bring people together into civil society in the first place. Second, Americans genuinely believed that others should come to enjoy the blessings of republican government which they had secured for themselves. There is something ironic in adopting with such moral fervor a republicanism based so much on the sturdy passions of self-preservation and self-interest yet the presence of such enthusiasm is undeniable. Americans greeted news of the French Revolution with strong feeling. The reception accorded France's Citizen Genet also stemmed from the sense of fellow-feeling. The belief in France as a champion of liberty meant, finally, a curious and potentially dangerous indifference to French ambitions in Europe and even for Louisiana. This enthusiasm for French republicanism did not come simply from a disinterested desire to see another's welfare improve, but neither did it spring simply from self-interest.

There were, however, limits to identifying the American purpose in the world simply as the promotion of human rights. First, there was the very real problem of the limited means available. The new republic simply did not have the capability to achieve much by way of promoting such rights. Hamilton and Jefferson were divided over the issue of how much power the United States possessed, but they each realized its limits.

Second, the law of nature when applied to nations led to restraint rather than excess on this question. The incorporation of Hobbes' teaching on natural rights and of sovereignty into the law of nations by Puffendorf and Vattel meant the movement in just-war theory from punishment to self-defense. Grotius had defended the action of a prince who went to war to defend citizens from the tyranny of their rulers, but the introduction of the theory of sovereignty based on natural rights made such action illegitimate. The sovereign rights of others meant that one state could not be the judge of what was best for another. When applied to states, then, the law of nature tended to define virtue as non-intervention.

This meant that the internal order within a state was not a legitimate object of concern among other states, except insofar as that state threatened its neighbors. On the other hand, the new conception of the law of nations expanded the right of revolution. The sovereign derived his authority from those who had entered the social contract: they could overthrow a tyrannical sovereign because the ruler's right to govern was limited by the original contract, which was broken by tyranny. Alexander Hamilton summarized the point this way:

51

To assist a people in a reasonable and virtuous struggle for liberty already begun, is both justifiable and laudable; but to incite to revolution everywhere, by indiscriminate offers of assistance before hand, is to invade and endanger the foundations of social tranquility."[18]

This teaching, among other things, meant the possibility, even the duty of neutrality which provided the authority for the policy of neutrality laid out by the Washington administration in the 1790's. It also meant that judging the probability of success was an important consideration in making policy. Since the state was the primary agent for securing individual rights, its duties to itself required more circumspection and care than those of an individual to himself. American support for human rights would have to be consistent with American honor and prosperity.

It was in accordance with these principles that Hamilton defended neutrality on moral, legal, and political grounds. Morally, nonintervention was the norm; legally, France had attacked first, thereby making inoperable the American treaty obligation to defend the French West Indies; and politically, it would have been imprudent to stake the existence of the United States for such inconsequential objects as the French West Indies. Beyond these points, however, Hamilton made it clear that he regarded France as the unjust power in the war:

There is no principle better supported by the doctrines of writers, the practice of nations, and the dictates of right reason, than this—that whenever a nation adopts maxims of conduct tending to the disturbance of the tranquility and established order of its neighbors, or manifesting a spirit of self-aggrandisement—it is lawful for other nations to combine against it, and, by force, to control the effects of those maxims and that spirit. The conduct of France, in instances which have been stated, calmly and impartially viewed, was an offence against the law of nations, which naturally made it a common cause among them to check her career.[19]

Morally, American liberty was founded with due respect for property, personal security, and religion. In their Revolution, the Americans exercised moderation and then, "without tumult or bloodshed," adopted a form of government which established "the foundations of Liberty on the basis of Justice, Order and Law."[20] All this stood in stark contrast with the licentiousness, anarchy, and atheism characteristic of French republicanism and Hamilton was anxious to make a clear distinction between the two. Practically, the "cause of liberty," which American Francophiles saw as indivisible, could be defeated in France but probably not in America. Should the Europeans defeat France and restore the monarchy, there would be all sorts of obstacles they would have to overcome to do the same in America, not the least of which would be each other. The operation of the balance of power system in Europe and the mutual jealously of France, Spain, and Britain would assure the Americans their independence. The danger of identifying French and American liberty was that such an identification might create the pretext the Europeans would otherwise lack for acting against the United States. This was all the more reason to stay out of European affairs as much as possible. In short, Hamilton did not rule out the cause of liberty as a reason to fight, but he did attach a moral and prudential calculus of success as part of the process.

A third restraint on American enthusiasm would be the readiness of others for the kinds of republican institutions which the Americans thought were best. While many Americans agreed in the abstract that a republican government was the best form of government for all, they also thought that not every nation was ready for it. Many of the favorable circumstances which made republican government possible in the United States were not present elsewhere. Both Hamilton and Jefferson were skeptical of the prospects for an American-style constitution for France, and both thought that the monarchy should continue to play a major, if limited, role in the French Constitution. As the American ambassador to France, Jefferson had a special vantage point to watch the unfolding of the French Revolution and to play a part in the making of the new Constitution. His suggestions are remarkable for their tolerance of the French monarchy from one with such an anti-monarchical bent.[21]

In an exchange with Lafayette in 1798-1799, Hamilton expressed his doubts that republicanism would succeed in France. He did not think that the French spirit or ethos could sustain such government.

> I shall only say that I hold with Montesquieu that a Government must be fitted to a nation as much as a Coat to the Individual, and consequently that what may be good at Philadelphia may be bad at Paris and ridiculous at Petersburgh.[22]

Hamilton demonstrated this "fitting" in the case of Santo Domingo as well. During the quasi-war with France, Hamilton and the American ambassador to Britain, Rufus King, considered forming a kind of condominium with the British to remove Spain, which had made peace with France in 1795, from the Western Hemisphere. In addition to the military arrangements, some agreement would be necessary as well on the forms of government which the two countries would sponsor or guarantee in place of Spanish rule. Secretary of State Pickering raised this issue with respect to the specific case of Santo Domingo, which had just declared its independence from France under Toussaint L'Ouverture and which sought trade and recognition from the government of the United States. Pickering asked Hamilton what kind of government ought to be established there. Hamilton's reply showed that he did not think that republicanism was possible in Santo Domingo either. "No regular system of liberty will at present suit." Instead he proposed a military government with a single executive to hold office for life, with his successor chosen by the rest of the military commanders. All males would be required to do military duty; laws and taxes were to be proposed by the executive to a military assembly composed of the generals and commanders of the regiments for their sanction or rejection. All of these recommendations "partake of the feudal system," which was the legacy of colonial rule in the West Indies.[23]

Indirect promotion of human rights

All of these checks on the possibility of the spread of human rights still left open the possibility of indirect assistance to human rights. One contributor was the balance of power system itself; the other was the success of the American experiment.

The relative self-sufficiency of the state meant that political association between nations was much less necessary than association between individuals. The law of nature did not require world government, as some of Vattel's predecessors had suggested. Instead a balance of power system could secure the rights established in the law of nations.

Modern Europe had become, according to Vattel, "a kind of republic, of which the members—each independent, but all linked together by the ties of common interest—unite for the maintenance of order and liberty."[24] The incorporation of the theory of sovereignty into the law of nations provided a basis in right for the basic aim of the balance of power system, namely the assurance of the survival of independent states.[25]

The Enlightenment science of the law of nations identified the alternative, universal monarchy, with world tyranny. An arrangement based on the existence of several independent loci of power and authority, though it could not ensure peace, still presented fewer evils. David Hume wrote fearfully of the consequences of universal monarchy where a religious class combined with a powerful monarchy to oppress the world.[26] The balance of power system presented the possibility that at least some of humankind could experience a modicum of security and comfort; it also meant that there would be a safe haven in other states for those fleeing persecution in their own.[27]

In addition, it was argued that the balance of power system would indirectly encourage the growth of liberalism within the states in the system. Checking the universalist claims of absolutist monarchies abroad would encourage a limitation of pretensions at home. Since large states were prone to despotism, the balance of power system would also check their size. One contribution the Americans could make to human rights, then, was to begin to contain the European states by removing themselves from the European system. In Europe's unchecked colonial expansions it has assumed unwarranted pretensions about its right to rule the earth. In consequence, as George Washington put it in his Farewell Address, one finds in European politics "ambition, rivalship, interest, humor, and caprice" so different from American prudence and sober republicanism. Washington asserted the need for a respectable defensive posture and held out the prospect that in the future the United States would have the power to defend its neutral rights. Earlier, in Federalist 11, Hamilton had gone further:

> Europe, by her arms and by her negotiations, by force and by fraud, has in different degrees exerted her dominion over them all. Africa, Asia, and America have successively felt her domination. The superiority she has long maintained has tempted her to plume herself as the mistress of the world, and to consider the rest of mankind as created for her benefit . . . It belongs to us to vindicate the honor of the human race, and to teach that assuming brother moderation.[28]

Finally the interaction of states within the balance of power system would encourage the exchange of trade and ideas which, too, would lead to moderation at home and better prospects for human rights. Commerce could contribute to human rights in at least two ways: first, a commercial focus might redirect human aggressions. Second, commerce depended on expanded property rights and on increased exchanges with foreigners. Hamilton defended the civilizing character of commerce in defending the Jay Treaty which included a prohibition of the sequestering of private property in war. This was one occasion where Hamilton found himself opposed by the authorities on the law of nations. The Romans, for example, allowed the right to sequester private property of foreigners but since they were a warlike rather than a commercial people they "carried the rights of war to an extreme not softened or humanized by the influence of commerce." The Romans even permitted the killing of foreign women and children in their midst during war: "What respect is due to maxims which have so inhuman a foundation?"[29]

Grotius and Vattel seemed to accept the Roman precedent, though with qualifications. Their contradictory opinions reflected their ambivalence about modern principles of commerce and civil law. Hamilton based his opposition to these jurists on the grounds of the customary law and the necessary law of nations. Noting the difference between ancient and modern practice on this point, Hamilton commented:

> At present in regard to the advantage and safety of commerce all the sovereigns of Europe have departed from this rigor. And as this custom has been generally received he who should act contrary to it would injure the public faith; for strangers trusted his subjects only from the firm persuasion that the general custom would be observed.[30]

Did the customary law bind the United States? Yes, through their connection with the British Empire and their acceptance of the common law. Ultimately, however, the customary law was derived from the law of nature: the obligation of nations to act with good faith to strangers who come into their midst with the understanding that they will be protected. Thus: "I derive the vindication of the article from a higher source; from the natural or necessary law of nations, from the eternal principles of morality and good faith."[31]

Finally, the success of the American experiment as a model republic would also contribute to the spread of human rights. Albert Gallatin argued during the Mexican War that the American mission "is to improve the state of the world, to be the 'model republic' to show that men are capable of governing themselves, and that this simple and natural form of government is also that which confers most happiness to all."[32]

57

NOTES

1. Richard Cox has suggested this point in his essay on Grotius in *History of Political Philosophy*, eds. Joseph Cropsey and Leo Strauss (2d. ed; Chicago: Rand McNally, 1972), pp. 360-361.

2. Friedrich von Gentz, "The French and American Revolutions Compared," trans. John Quincy Adams *Three Revolutions*, ed., Stefan Possony (Chicago: Henry Regnery, 1959), pp. 3-95.

3. Quoted in Gerald Stourzh, *Alexander Hamilton and the Idea of Republican Government* (Stanford: Stanford University Press, 1970), p. 12.

4. "Full Vindication of the Measures of Congress," *The Papers of Alexander Hamilton*, eds. Jacob Cooke and Harold Syrett (26 vols.; New York: Columbia University Press), I, pp. 45-78.

5. "Remarks on the Treaty of Amity, Commerce, and Navigation Lately Made with Great Britain," *Hamilton Papers*, XVIII, p. 415.

6. Thomas Jefferson, "A Summary View of the Rights of British North America," in *The Papers of Thomas Jefferson*, ed. Julian Boyd (x vols.; Princeton: Princeton University Press, 1950), I, p. 121.

7. Gentz, p. 71.

8. "A Full Vindication of the Measures of Congress," *Hamilton Papers*, I, pp. 45-78.

9. "Considerations on the Nature and Extent of the Legislative Authority of the British Parliament," *The Works of James Wilson*, ed. James DeWitt Andrews (2 vols.; Chicago: Callaghan and Co., 1896), II, p. 506.

10. "The Farmer Refuted," *Hamilton Papers*, I, pp. 87-88.

11. "To the New York *Evening Post*," *Hamilton Papers*, XXV, p. 536.

12. Burlamaqui, *The Principles of Natural and Politic Law* (Reprint; 2 vols.; New York: Arno Press, 1972), II, p. 73.

13. Ibid.

14. "Speech at the Convention at Philadelphia," *Works*, II, p. 545.

15. Alexander Hamilton, James Madison, and John Jay, *The Federalist Papers*, intro. Clinton Rossiter (New York: New American Library, 1961), p. 73.

16. Ibid., p. 83.

17. John Quincy Adams, *The Lives of James Madison and James Monroe* (Buffalo: George H. Derby and Co., 1850), p. 33.

18. Hamilton, "The Stand, No. 2," *Hamilton Papers*, XVIII, p. 394.

19. Hamilton, "Remarks on the Treaty of Amity, Commerce, and Navigation Lately Made with Great Britain," *Hamilton Papers*, XVIII, p. 424.

20. "Americanus, No. 2," *Hamilton Papers*, X.

21. See *Jefferson Papers*.

22. Hamilton to Lafayette, Jan. 6, 1799, *Hamilton Papers*, XII, p. 404.

23. Pickering to Hamilton, Feb. 9, 1799 and Hamilton to Pickering, Feb. 21, 1799, *Hamilton Papers*, XXII, pp. 473-475 and 492-493.

24. Emmerich de Vattel, *The Law of Nations*, trans. Joseph Chitty (6th ed.; Philadelphia: T. and J. W. Johnson, 1844), Bk. III, ch. 3, sect. 47.

25. Edward Gulick, *Europe's Classical Balance of Power* (New York: W. W. Norton, 1955), p. 30.

26. David Hume, "Of the Balance of Power," *Philosophical Works*, eds, T. H. Green and T. H. Grose (4 vols.; Darmstadt: Scientia Verlag Allen, 1964), I, pp. 353-356.

27. Charles Davenant, *Essays Upon the Balance of Power*, (London: James Knapton, 1701), pp. 277-283.

28. See *The Federalist Papers*, pp. 90-91.

29. Alexander Hamilton, "The Defense, No. 20," *Hamilton Papers*, XIX, pp. 329-333.

30. "The Defense," No. 21, *ibid.*, p. 372.

31. *Ibid*, p. 342.

32. Albert Gallatin, "The Mission of the United States," *Selected Writings of Albert Gallatin*, ed. E. James Ferguson (New York: Bobbs-Merrill, 1976), p. 485.

TRADITION, THE FOUNDING FATHERS, AND FOREIGN AFFAIRS

Norman A. Graebner

Traditions rest lightly on the American people. With the founding of the Republic 200 years ago Americans, contemplating the rich continent before them as well as the possibilities afforded by their new Constitution, could anticipate one long experiment in free government and economic progress unrestrained by the lessons of history. Through succeeding generations citizens of the United States have generally detected little need for historic guidance in the formulation of attitudes, purposes, and policies. Even intellectual conservatives often reveal little respect for the nation's past. Still there is now a wide-spread lament, shared by writers, scholars, and political leaders, that the country lacks a tradition in foreign affairs commensurate with its power and responsibilities. The only diplomatic tradition widely recognized is that of Woodrow Wilson, but Wilson's views partook of the very exceptionalism that denied the need for examining the past for guidance. Regarding power politics as an unacceptable, even immoral, foundation for the country's external policies, Wilson insisted that the United States should not and need not follow the rules of traditional diplomacy. Those who reject the Wilsonian approach to international affairs often express regret that the country lacks a countering American tradition which might serve as a more effective and realistic guide to national action abroad.

This is strange. The Founding Fathers whom we celebrate in this bicentennial season were themselves the creatures of tradition, steeped in the political and diplomatic wisdom of the age. Overwhelmingly the nation's early leaders accepted the philosophic conviction of Edmund

Burke, the noted eighteenth-century English writer and statesman, that society comprised a continuing compact between the dead, the living, and the yet unborn. The living might be masters of their immediate destiny, but they would, if they were wise, take cognizance of those traditions that had the sanction of wisdom and common sense and transmit that heritage to those who would follow. In fulfilling that obligation to themselves and to posterity such early Americans as George Washington, Thomas Jefferson, James Madison, Alexander Hamilton, John and John Quincy Adams, in their voluminous writings, drew on the past to create for the United States a diplomatic tradition unmatched in history.

Without exception the Founding Fathers recognized a world of power politics in which all nations were free to define and pursue their own interests, that in practice republics were no less addicted to war than monarchies. A world of national sovereignties, with each responsible only to itself, left little room for trust, except to trust that nations would be guided by their own interests. That fundamental principle permitted Washington to laud the alliance with France, although the United States was entrusting its destiny to Europe's most powerful monarchy. As Washington explained in November, 1778: "Hatred of England may carry some to excess of Confidence in France. . . . I am heartily disposed to entertain the most favourable sentiments of our new ally and to cherish them in others to a reasonable degree; but it is a maxim founded on the universal experience of mankind, that no nation is to be trusted farther than it is bound by its interest; and no prudent statesman or politician will venture to depart from it." When a British general chided the United States in the House of Commons for making an unnatural alliance with France, John Adams retorted: "I know of no better rule than this—when two nations have the same interests in general, they are natural allies; when they have opposite interests, they are natural enemies. . . . [But] the habits of affection or enmity between nations are easily changed as circumstances vary, and as essential interests alter." Like all alliances, Adams knew, that with France would be temporary, created only to satisfy an immediate mutual interest in the defeat of Great Britain. No less than

Washington and Adams, members of Congress welcomed the French alliance because they assumed the existence of strong mutual interests in the struggle against Britain. France, despite the freedom that came with great power, would do its duty to the infant United States.

For the Founding Fathers, no less than for European statesmen, the central task of diplomacy was that of limiting the behavior of the ambitious to what they regarded acceptable. What preserved Europe's remarkable stability, despite its continuing wars, was the existence of an equilibrium or balance of power. Nations checked the recurrent selfishness of others with counterchecks composed of opposing combinations of power. The Founding Fathers discovered early that the European equilibrium would be the essential source of American security. Even as colonists the American people achieved major victories over Europe's two most powerful countries by managing to throw British power against France to drive the French from the North American continent, and then, within twenty years, to drive the British out of the thirteen colonies by utilizing the power of France. Thereafter John Adams and Thomas Jefferson, representing the young Republic in London and Paris respectively, understood clearly that as long as Britain and France, occupying the two poles of the European equilibrium, remained strong and antagonistic toward the other, the United States was safe. Neither London or Paris would permit the other to interfere in American affairs to the detriment of the European equilibrium. Thomas Boylston Adams, one of the sons of John Adams, expressed this truth in October, 1799: "It must always happen, so long as America is an independent Republic or nation, that the balance of power in Europe will continue to be of the utmost importance to her welfare. The moment that France is victorious and Great Britain with her allies depressed, we have cause for alarm ourselves. The same is true when the reverse of this happens."

None of the nation's early leaders matched Thomas Jefferson in his persistent concern for the European equilibrium. During his years as minister to France he commented often and brilliantly on Europe's shifting balance of power and its significance for European and Atlantic stability. With the outbreak of the Napoleonic wars after

1803, with the full might of Napoleon's France confronting that of Britain and the rest of Europe, Jefferson feared a victory of either France or Britain over the other. After Napoleon's triumph at Austerlitz in 1806 Jefferson, as President, considered an alliance with Britain. Soon British insolence forced him back into a posture of neutrality, although he continued to believe that the French emperor endangered the balance of power and thus the security of the United States. Jefferson wrote that he still favored "an English ascendancy on the ocean [as being] safer for us than that of France." In the wake of the *Chesapeake* affair of 1807, however, he confessed: "I never expected to be under the necessity of wishing success to Buonaparte. But the English being equally tyrannical at sea as he is on land, & the tyranny bearing on us in every point of either honor or interest, I say 'down with England' and as for what Buonaparte is then to do to us, let us trust to the chapter of accidents. I cannot with the Anglomen, prefer a certain present evil to a future hypothetical one."

Even as the United States entered its war against England in 1812, Jefferson believed that Napoleon, now America's informal ally, had grown too powerful and hoped that Britain, although the declared enemy of the United States, would find an opportunity for reducing its great rival. Jefferson wrote on that occasion: "We especially ought to pray that the powers of Europe may be so poised and counterpoised among themselves, that their own security may require the presence of all their forces at home, leaving the other quarters of the globe in undisturbed tranquility." Throughout the war it mattered less to Jefferson whether Britain or France triumphed in Europe than that the European equilibrium remained intact. He no more than the Adamses would entrust American security to the Atlantic alone.

If the pursuit of precisely defined and limited interests in a carefully balanced world of sovereign nations established the outlines of American foreign policy, the Founding Fathers faced powerful impediments to their closely calculated approach to world affairs. From the beginning the American people displayed a profound propensity to involve themselves in external affairs far beyond either their interests or their effective power. The

French Revolution quickly taught President Washington and his Federalist advisers that the country's republican ideology and revolutionary zeal, unleashed by the American Revolution itself, could readily encourage Americans to make other people's causes their own. When Washington attempted to maintain the official neutrality of the United States in the burgeoning war between France and the allied powers led by Britain, his political opponents accused him of ignoring the cause of liberty. Only with difficulty did the Washington administration prevent the country from mounting a futile crusade in behalf of the French.

Alexander Hamilton rushed to the defense of the Washington administration with a series of brilliant essays, published under the names "Pacificus" and "Americanus." These writings constituted the most pervading examination of the diplomatic principles guiding the young Republic to come from the pen of any of the nation's early leaders. What troubled Hamilton especially was the popular plea that the United States owed a debt of gratitude to France. In denying that gratitude could serve as a basis of external policy, Hamilton noted simply that governments could not operate as individuals. "Existing millions and for the most part future generations," he wrote, "are concerned in the present measures of a government: While the consequences of the private actions of an individual, for the most part, terminate with himself or are circumscribed within a narrow compass. Whence it follows, that an individual may on numerous occasions meritoriously indulge the emotions of generosity and benevolence; not only without an eye to, but even at the expense of his own interest. But a nation can rarely be justified in pursuing (a similar) course; and when it does so ought to confine itself within much stricter bounds."

Throughout his second term Washington was dismayed by the intense partisanship which too many Americans entertained toward the European belligerents. He stressed the necessity of greater attention to American interests in a letter to Patrick Henry: "My ardent desire is . . . to see that (the United States) *may be* independent of *all*, and under the influence of *none*. In a word, I want an *American* character, that the powers of Europe may be convinced we act for *ourselves* and not for *others* . . ." In his Farewell Address Washington explained why foreign attachments endangered the nation's well-being: "The Nation, which indulges toward another an habitual hatred, or an habitual fondness, is in some degree a slave. It is a slave to its animosity or its affection, either of which is sufficient to lead it astray from its duty and its interests." Sympathy for favored countries, Washington warned, assumed common interests which seldom existed and enmeshed a people in the enmities of others without justification.

John Quincy Adams, ultimately the greatest of all American diplomatists, assigned himself the special obligation to warn the nation against unnecessary and unpromising involvements in the affairs of others. When pro-French pressures mounted against the Washington administration in 1793, Adams wrote in his "Marcellus" papers: "As men, we must undoubtedly lament the effusion of human blood, and the mass of misery and distress which is preparing for the great part of the civilized world; but as the citizens of a nation at a vast distance from the continent of Europe, . . . disconnected from all European interests and European politics, it is our duty to remain, the peaceable and silent, though sorrowful spectators of the sanguinary scene." In December, 1817, as secretary of state, John Quincy Adams complained to his father that Latin America, then in revolution against Spain, had replaced France as the great external source of discord in the United States. "The republican spirit of our country," he wrote, "not only sympathizes with people struggling in a cause, . . . but it is working into indignation against the relapse of Europe into the opposite principle of monkery and despotism. And now, as at the early stage of the French Revolution, we have ardent spirits who are for rushing into the conflict, without looking to the consequences." When in 1821 enthusiasts, with no attention to means, sought to launch a crusade to save the Greeks from Turkish oppression, Adams again admonished his fellow Americans in his noted July 4 address of that year. "Wherever the standard of freedom and Independence has been or shall be unfurled," he said, "there will (America's) heart, her benedictions and her prayers be. But she goes not abroad, in search of monsters to destroy. She is the well-wisher to the freedom and independence of all. She is the champion and vindicator only of her own."

It was not strange that the Founding Fathers, facing recurrent pressures for foreign involvements which they opposed, preached isolationism. But even on that subject their thought was remarkably sophisticated. Washington, in his famed Farewell Address, acknowledged that distance and oceans are significant sources of security and power. Why not maximize such advantages by avoiding unnecessary involvements in other continents? When Washington reminded the American people that "Europe has a set of primacy interests which to us have none or very remote relation," he recognized the fact that the issues over which Europeans had fought for centuries were simply not the concern of the United States. Nowhere did the Farewell Address excuse the government of the United States from acting when the country's interests justified it. Indeed, the nation could choose, in Washington's words, "peace or war, as our interest, guided by justice, shall counsel."

This sampling of the thought of the Founding Fathers on foreign affairs cannot render full justice to the country's early leaders, but it should suffice to demonstrate again the quality of mind and elegance of expression that established their place in history. No aspect of international affairs escaped them. Every argument and every decision followed some established principle. Their warnings against overinvolvement, their preference for cooperative rather than unilateral action were historic and sound. If the precepts of the early Republic were lost on subsequent generations, the remarkable tradition they embody is ours to recall and ponder. This complex and difficult age in which we live demands no less.

THE IMPERIAL PRESIDENCY:
TWENTY YEARS AFTER

Arthur Schlesinger, Jr.

My title contains an echo of Dumas; but my tale, alas, is less ennobling. Still, like d'Artagnan and his three brave comrades, the Imperial Presidency in the United States has attempted a comeback almost two decades after the fall of Richard Nixon. The recent renewal of presidential aggrandizement and the current reaction against it invite us to recall the vicissitudes of the American presidency over these years—and to consider what lessons this experience may impart for the future.

The Imperial Presidency as a phenomenon goes back further, of course, than twenty years, though the phrase itself is hardly 14 years old. It was the title of a book written in the latter days, hectic and ominous, of the Nixon presidency and published toward the end of 1973. My argument in *The Imperial Presidency* was that the American Constitution intends a strong presidency within an equally strong system of accountability. My title referred to the condition that ensues when the constitutional balance between presidential power and presidential accountability is upset in favor of presidential power.

The perennial threat to the constitutional balance, I suggested, springs from foreign policy. Confronted by presidential initiatives at home, Congress and the courts—the countervailing branches of government under the American principle of the separation of powers—have robust confidence in their own information and judgment. In domestic policy the other branches do not lightly surrender power to the executive. But confronted by presidential initiatives abroad, Congress and the courts, along with the press and the citizenry too, generally lack confidence in their information and judgment. In foreign policy the disposition has consequently been to hand over power and responsibility to the President.

The great French observer Tocqueville foresaw all this a century and a half ago. "It is chiefly in its foreign relations," he wrote, "that the executive power of a nation finds occasion to exert its skill and its strength. If the existence of the American Union were perpetually threatened, if its chief interests were in daily connection with those of other powerful nations, the executive would assume an increased importance." But the nation that Tocqueville inspected in the 1830s existed in happy isolation from world power conflicts. So, he observed, "the President of the United States possesses almost royal prerogatives which he has no opportunity of exercising."[1]

The presidency had always flourished in times of war. "We elect a king every four years," Secretary of State William H. Seward told the *London Times* correspondent during the Civil War, "and give him absolute power within certain limits, which after all he can interpret for himself."[2] But in the past peace has brought reaction against executive excess. Within a dozen years Seward's elective-kingship theory faded away, and the new era was famously characterized by Professor Woodrow Wilson as one of "congressional government."

Then after 1898 the Spanish-American War stimulated a flow of power back to the presidency. In his preface to the 15th edition in 1901, the author of *Congressional Government* himself called attention to "the greatly increased power . . . given the President by the plunge into international politics." When foreign policy becomes the nation's dominant concern, Wilson said, the executive "must of necessity be its guide: must utter every initial judgment, take every first step of action, supply the information upon which it is to act, suggest and in large measure control its conduct."[3] In another fifteen years the First World War gave Wilson, now President himself, the opportunity to exercise those almost royal prerogatives. Once again the elective kingship faded away. Post-war disillusion revived congressional assertiveness. In the 1930s Franklin Roosevelt, a mighty domestic President, could not stop Congress from enacting the rigid neutrality legislation that put American foreign policy in a straitjacket while Hitler ran amok in Europe.

Since Pearl Harbor, however, Americans have lived under a conviction of international crisis, sustained, chronic and often interse. The republic is at last fully in the age foreseen by Tocqueville: American interests are in daily connection with those of other powerful states, the nation seems perpetually threatened and Presidents freely exercise their almost royal prerogatives. In the last forty years the Imperial Presidency, once a transient wartime phenomenon, has become to a degree, at least institutionalized.

The most palpable index of executive aggrandizement is the transfer of the power to go to war from Congress, where the Constitution expressly lodged it, to the presidency. In the bitter month of June 1940, when Paul Reynaud pleaded for American aid against Hitler's *Blitzkrieg*, Franklin Roosevelt, after saying that the United States could continue supplies so long as France continued resistance, took care to add: "These statements carry with them no implication of military commitments. Only the Congress can make such commitments."[4] How old-fashioned this sentiment sounds today! In another year Roosevelt himself sent the American Navy into an undeclared war in the North Atlantic, though he did not claim inherent presidential power to do so. In another decade, when President Truman committed American forces to war in Korea, he asserted just that claim. Presidents Johnson, Nixon and Reagan thereafter assumed that the power to send troops into combat is an inherent right of the presidency and does not require congressional authorization.

Nixon carried presidential prerogative too far, however, when he took the powers flowing to the presidency from international crisis and turned them against his political opponents at home. In Nixon's hands the claim to inherent presidential power swelled into the delusion that the presidency was above the law and the Constitution. I recognize that the Watergate affair is imperfectly understood here in France, but this was the issue as Americans saw it; and the consequence of Watergate on the heels of the Vietnam War was to provoke the reaction in the 1970s against the Imperial Presidency.

Congress, seized by a temporary passion to prevent future Vietnams and Watergates, enacted laws designed to reclaim lost powers, to dismantle the executive secrecy system and to ensure future presidential accountability. The War Powers Act of 1973 was meant to restrain the presidential inclination to go to war. A variety of laws limited presidential resort to paramilitary and covert action. Congress set up select committees to monitor the Central Intelligence Agency. It gave the Freedom of Information Act new vitality. It imposed its own priorities—human rights and nuclear non-proliferation, for example—on the executive foreign policy. The Congressional Budget Act of 1974 restricted the presidential authority to impound appropriations voted by Congress. The National Emergencies Act of 1976 terminated existing presidential emergency authority and established congressional review for future national-emergency declarations. Legislative vetoes and reporting requirements curtailed presidential freedom of action in a diversity of fields.

For a season the presidency appeared in rout. Vietnam had driven Johnson from the White House. Nixon had driven himself. Nixon's successors—the hapless Gerald Ford and the hapless Jimmy Carter—proved incapable of mastering the discordant frustrations of the day. These four Presidents came from both parties, from a variety of cultural backgrounds and from diverse sections of the country. The fact that four such different men all failed in the presidency led some observers to believe that the fault lay not in the individuals occupying the office but in the office itself.

In 1973 the concern had been the excessive power claimed by a President as his inherent right. By the end of the 1970s the republic was consumed by an opposite concern—that the presidency had become too weak to do the job. This was a time of despair about the presidency. Columnists wrote of "the presidency in decline." Political scientists produced books under such titles as *The Tethered Presidency, The Impossible Presidency, The Illusion of Presidential Power.* Pundits confidently predicted an age of one-term presidents. The impression arose of a beleaguered and pathetic fellow sitting impotently in the Oval Office, assailed by unprecedently intractable problems, paralyzed by the constitutional separation of powers, hemmed in by congressional and bureaucratic constraints, pushed one way or another by exigent special-interest groups, seduced, betrayed and abandoned by the mass media. The once mighty American presidency appeared tied down, like Gulliver, by a web of debilitating statutory and political bonds. In 1980 ex-President Ford said to general applause, "We have not an imperial presidency but an imperilled presidency."[5]

Half a dozen years later concern has shifted back from presidential weakness to presidential power. President Reagan demonstrated that the presidency was far from an insolvent office. Contrary to the expectations of the late 1970s, he won easy reelection to a second term. The congressional reclamation of power after Watergate turned out to be largely make-believe. The War Powers Act had no effect in restraining presidents from sending troops into combat, whether in Lebanon or in Grenada or in Libya. The Congressional Budget Act became an instrument that the President successfully turned against Congress. Reagan reestablished the executive secrecy system. He brought the CIA back from its season of disgrace, made it once again the President's private army and sent it off, without congressional approval, to overthrow the government of Nicaragua.

In order to escape the CIA's nominal obligation to report its dark deeds to congressional oversight committees and in order to evade the laws of the land, Reagan converted the National Security Council, heretofore a policy-coordination body, into an operating agency and permitted it to indulge in the now notorious Iran-Contra flimflam. Having placed the integrity and credibility of the United States in the hands of Iranian confidence men, the administration made exposure inevitable; and, when the inevitable exposure began, the administration took refuge in a bluster of incomplete, misleading and, on occasion, false accounts of what its members had wrought. In the meantime, the scheme violated not only standards of intelligence and responsibility in the conduct of foreign affairs but very likely also the Export Administration Act, the Arms Export Control Act, the Omnibus Anti-Terrorism

Act, the National Security Act, the Boland Amendment and
the Neutrality Act.

No doubt the very size of his victory in 1984
contributed to President Reagan's subsequent difficulties.
Every President in modern times who won election with
more than 60 per cent of the popular vote has found
himself in trouble soon thereafter. So Warren G. Harding
(60.4 percent in 1920) moved on from triumph to Teapot
Dome; Franklin D. Roosevelt (60.8 percent in 1936) to the
court-packing plan; Lyndon Johnson (61.1 percent in 1964) to
Vietnam; Richard Nixon (60.7 percent in 1972) to the
Watergate cover-up. Since Reagan fell a little short of 60
percent in 1984, he might have been exempt from the
general rule, but his luck at last has failed him. Having
misread a gratifying electoral success as a grant of
immunity for the rest of his term in office, he overreached,
like his eminent predecessors, and is now reaping the
whirlwind.

The euphoria induced by too large a margin of victory
appears to loosen the presidential grasp on reality. Reagan
and his White House staff evidently supposed that the
election sweep empowered them to do whatever they thought
necessary for the safety of the republic without regard to
obligations imposed by the Constitution or by the statute
book. They considered secrecy an all-embracing presidential
protection and entitlement, even when its purpose was to
escape the accountability that is the essence of the
constitutional system. The Reagan presidency has upset the
constitutional balance between presidential power and
presidential accountability and has thereby provoked the
movement we see today to restore the constitutional
balance.

The reaction against executive usurpation is already, as
it did after Watergate, provoking a counter-reaction. We
are beginning to hear again that the presidency itself is in
danger. We are told once more that too zealous an inquiry
into executive abuses will cripple the presidential office.
The prospect of a fifth consecutive failed presidency is
leading some to conclude that the fatal flaw lies not in the
individuals occupying the office but in the office itself. I
beg you not to be unduly impressed by these gloomy
apprehensions.

In the short run, if a President is inclined to do foolish things, surely a crippled presidency is better for the nation and the world than an unrepentant and unchastened one. And the crippling of a President who does foolish things does not mean a crippling of the presidential office. The reaction against Watergate did not prevent Reagan from having a successful first term, nor would it have handicapped Ford and Carter had they been more competent in the job.

Nor can one conclude from another failed presidency that there is something basically wrong with the system. The Constitution has never pretended to guarantee against presidential incompetence, folly, stupidity or criminality. As the Supreme Court once said in a celebrated decision, the republic has "no right to expect that it will always have wise and humane rulers, sincerely attached to the principles of the Constitution. Wicked men, ambitious of power, with hatred of liberty and contempt of law, may fill the place once occupied by Washington and Lincoln."[6]

The Constitution cannot guarantee against that. But, through the principle of the separation of powers, it can guarantee that, when a President abuses power, corrective forces exist to redress the constitutional balance. As Senator Sam Ervin put it in Watergate days, "One of the great advantages of the three separate branches of government is that it's difficult to corrupt all three at the same time."[7] The press, as a *de facto* fourth branch, serves as a powerful reinforcement of the corrective process. No doubt it is hard for those accustomed to the fusion of powers characteristic of the parliamentary system to grasp the dialectical workings of a system founded on the separation of powers. Still to each his own; and, as Justice Brandeis said, the point of the American system is "not to promote efficiency but to preclude the exercise of arbitrary power."[8]

The present reaction against Reaganite excess is surely not a failure but a vindication of American democracy. It is evidence of the determination of the American people to defend the rule of law. It is an admonition to future presidents to respect the oath they take at their inauguration to execute the office faithfully and to preserve and protect the Constitution.

I recognize that they order things differently in France. The secret services can attack the blameless *Greenpeace*, and no one seems to care whether the President and Prime Minister authorized the action. From this perspective, American concern over the Iran-Nicaragua flimflam, like American concern over Watergate, may seem mystifying. Why should the world's most powerful democracy engage in so spectacular act of self-immolation over so inconsequential an affair as this? But the issue is not the scheme to get the Ayatollah to subsidize the Contras, nor even its Inspector Clouseau mode of execution. The issue is whether the President of the United States is above the Constitution and the laws.

I remember the English historian Hugh Trevor-Roper explaining Watergate to a British audience by comparing it with the revolt against royal prerogative in 17th century England. When Hampden refused to pay ship-money in 1636, the real issue went far beyond ship-money to the crown's claim to absolute power. Foreigners wondered why the English made such a fuss about ship-money when an unhampered English government might have been effective in Europe. "But the English," Trevor-Roper wrote, "thought first of their own liberties; and who shall say that they were wrong?"[9]

Nor need anyone fear that the recurrent uproar against the Imperial Presidency will inflict permanent damage on the office. For the American presidency, I assure you, is indestructible. This is partly so for functional reasons. The separation of powers among three supposedly equal and coordinate branches of government creates an inherent tendency toward inertia and stalemate. One of the three branches must take the initiative if the system is to move. The executive branch alone is structurally capable of taking that initiative. The men who framed the Constitution intended that it should do so. "Energy in the Executive," as Alexander Hamilton put it in the Federalist Papers, "is a leading character in the definition of good government."[10]

Moreover, the growth of presidential initiative has resulted less from presidential rapacity for power than from the necessities of governing an ever more complex society. As a tiny agricultural country, straggling along the Atlantic seaboard, turned into a mighty continental, industrial and finally world power, the problems assailing the national polity increased vastly in number, size and urgency. Most of these problems could not be tackled without vigorous executive leadership. Through American history, a strong presidency has kept the system in motion. The President remains, as Woodrow Wilson said, "the only national voice," the presidency "the vital place of action in the system."[11]

A third reason for the indestructibility of the presidency lies in the psychology of mass democracy. Once again Tocqueville provides the text. "Our contemporaries," he wrote, "are constantly excited by two conflicting passions: they want to be led, and they wish to remain free. . . . By this system the people shake off their dependency just long enough to select their master and then relapse into it again."[12] Americans have always had considerable ambivalence about the presidency. One year they denounce presidential despotism. The next they demand presidential leadership. While they are quite proficient at cursing out presidents—a proficiency that helps keep the system in balance—they also have a profound longing to believe in and admire them. Reagan's success in his first term expressed a widespread national desire for presidents to succeed, even when he proposed policies that made little sense and to which in many cases, if public opinion polls can be believed, a majority of Americans were opposed.

The presidency will survive. Its mighty powers lie ready to be mobilized by any leader prepared to operate within the Constitution and to persuade Congress that his course is right. But, when presidents abuse their powers, they can expect retribution, even when it causes a temporary impasse in foreign policy. Americans think first of their own liberties, and who shall say that they are wrong?

Still a further question must be considered: what leads American presidents into the imperial temptation? Can we expect reversions to the Imperial Presidency in the future? If so, does this mean a fundamental weakness in the structure of the American polity? But we have already noted that no system can insure against wicked men filling the place once occupied by Washington and Lincoln. The problem is not so cosmic. It is rather that of isolating what it is that lures a President who is not a wicked man into abusing his power. The answer, I judge, lies not in the structure of polity but in the purpose of policy.

For in recent times the United States has been subject to periodic delusions that the national mission is to redeem a fallen world. The real question is whether a global and messianic foreign policy is compatible with the American Constitution. When the American presidency conceives itself as the appointed savior of a world in which mortal danger requires rapid and incessant deployment of men, weapons and decisions behind a wall of secrecy, power rushes from Capitol Hill to the White House. This is what has happened at critical moments in the years since Pearl Harbor. As long ago as 1967, an apprehensive Senate Judiciary Committee established a Subcommittee on Separation of Powers under the redoubtable chairmanship of Senator Ervin. Six years later the Ervin Subcommittee declared that "the movement of the United States into the forefront of balance-of-power realpolitik in international matters has been accomplished at the cost of the internal balance-of-power painstakingly established by the Constitution."[13]

Whether this was a necessary cost the Subcommittee did not say. It would be excessively gloomy, however, to suppose that a prudent balance-of-power foreign policy confined to vital interests of the United States is irreconcilable with the separation of powers. An imprudent foreign policy, however, aiming at the salvation of the world and involving the United States in useless wars and grandiose dreams, is another matter. Vietnam and Iran/Nicaragua were the direct consequences of global messianism, Watergate an indirect consequence.

The Imperial Presidency is essentially the creation of foreign policy. As I wrote a dozen or so years ago, "A combination of doctrines and emotions—a belief in permanent and universal crisis, fear of communism, faith in the duty and the right of the United States to intervene swiftly in every part of the world—had brought about the unprecedented decisions over war and peace in the presidency. With this there came an unprecedented exclusion of the rest of the executive branch, of Congress, of the press and of public opinion in general from these decisions. . . . So the Imperial Presidency grew at the expense of the constitutional order. Like the cowbird, it hatched its own eggs and pushed the others out of the nest."[14]

This diagnosis still seems valid to me. If a messianic foreign policy is essential to the future of the United States, then the United States must have a new constitution. But I do not think that we need abandon that noble document. And, if a messianic foreign policy bursts the limits of the Constitution, then the wisdom of the Framers is even greater than one could have imagined, for such a foreign policy is hopeless on its merits and can only bring disaster to the American republic. The best insurance against a revival of the Imperial Presidency would be the revival of realism, sobriety and responsibility in the conduct of foreign affairs.

In the meantime, the tug-of-war between Congress and the executive will continue. In this continuing struggle, the advantage will lie with the president so long as he respects the Constitution and the laws and so long as his policies command general assent. Once a president embarks on reckless policies in defiance of the Constitution and the laws, he can expect precisely what is happening to President Reagan today. No one should be dismayed at the process. It is the way the American democracy stays healthy. The world will be better off for it in the long run, and very likely in the short run too.

NOTES

1. Alexis de Tocqueville, *Democracy in America*, I, ch. viii.

2. Louis Jennings, *Eighty Years of Republican Government in the United States* (London, 1868), p. 36.

3. Woodrow Wilson, *Congressional Government* (15th Ed., Boston, 1901), pp. xi-xii.

4. W. L. Langer and S. E. Gleason, *The Challenge to Isolation* (New York, 1952), p. 539.

5. Gerald R. Ford, "Imperilled, not Imperial," *Time*, 10 November 1980.

6. *Ex Parte Milligan*, 4 Wall 2, 125 (1866).

7. John M. Blume, et al, *The National Experience* (6th ed., San Diego, 1985), pp. 862-864.

8. *Myers v. United States*, 272 U.S. 52, 293, (1926).

9. Hugh Trevor-Roper, "Nixon—America's Charles I?", *Spectator*, 11 August 1973.

10. 70th Federalist.

11. Woodrow Wilson, *Constitutional Government in the United States* (New York, 1908), pp. 68, 73.

12. Tocqueville, *Democracy in America*, II, Fourth Book, ch. vi.

13. Separation of Powers Subcommittee, *Congressional Oversight of Executive Agreements*, 93 Cong, 1 Sess. (1973), p. 1.

14. Arthur M. Schlesinger, Jr., *The Imperial Presidency* (Boston, 1973), p. 208.

A MIND WITH FEW LIMITS

Hugh Sidey

By the reckoning of Dumas Malone, the world's preeminent Jeffersonian biographer, "No other American document has been read so often or listened to by so many weary and perspiring audiences" as the Declaration of Independence. Certainly new records were set this Fourth as the words of Thomas Jefferson about "self-evident" truths and "unalienable rights" were beamed from the base of the Statue of Liberty around the globe. "Those well-worn phrases have never lost their potency and charm," insists Malone, though at the time they were first introduced, Jefferson was still miffed that his original text had been edited by the Continental Congress. Jefferson was not even in the limelight. He was poking around Philadelphia, buying a thermometer and seven pairs of ladies' gloves before going home to Monticello. Years later, he said his intention had been "to place before mankind the common sense of the subject." Jefferson, as much as any man of his time, believes Malone, had already focused on the future and was deeply concerned about the daunting task of translating the Declaration into "legal institutions." Two centuries later, we still struggle at the job.

Many Americans back then gloried in the Jeffersonian eloquence, then turned away from the tasks it prescribed for them. Too many Americans still do that, says Malone, who is 94, and spent 50 years completing his six volumes on Jefferson, 5 1/2 of which follow the events that came after the moment of creation in July 1776. Common sense about the things that still plague mankind flowed from Jefferson's extraordinary pen for half a century after that date in papers, letters and laws.

Scholars know about Jefferson's insistence that "the earth belongs to the living, not to the dead," and how he wanted that principle applied to eliminating national debts, particularly war debts. But few practitioners of today's politics have read those admonitions. Jefferson contended that one generation, which he meticulously calculated from the rough data available to run about 19 years, should not unreasonably burden its successors. He believed sufficient taxes should be levied to clear the books in that 19-year stretch so that a new generation could face its own problems unencumbered. That pay-as-you-go principle might also be an effective restraint on the "dog of war," reasoned Jefferson, who had seen the European potentates suffocate their subjects with debt from wars of pride and whim.

Jefferson's marvelous mind knew few limits. Laws of a nation and even constitutions should undergo generational revisions, he suggested. "No society can make a perpetual constitution, or even a perpetual law," he wrote. He felt, like few other men of his age, the inexorable current of humankind in which the only constant was change. But, of course, he was too much the dreamer. His friend James Madison brought him down to earth, pointing out that generations were not mere tidy mathematical certainties and that debts, like those incurred for the American Revolution, could benefit those who were to come. As always, Jefferson acknowledged the wisdom of Madison's view, but he could never rid himself of the feeling that unrestrained debt was as great an enemy of "natural rights" as King George III.

It is notable in this the week after the great party that among the questions facing the U.S. are these: What right do we have to pile up a $2 trillion debt for our children to pay? How can we in good conscience indulge desires that may leave the earth poisoned and exhausted within a few decades? Why, if we must spend $300 billion for our war machine, should we not use taxes to pay for that burden in our time?

Thomas Jefferson is whispering to us to read on.

WHAT WOULD JEFFERSON SAY?

Hugh Sidey

It is a good time to get away from Washington and ask one of the old hands like Thomas Jefferson how the country looks from where he reposes. Jefferson is in style more than ever—the man who suspected bigness, distrusted cities, believed passionately in individuality. Jefferson is not readily available for consultation, of course. But if one cannot talk to him, then Dumas Malone, the pre-eminent biographer, can stand in.

"I feel more at home here than anywhere," said the historian as he went up the hill to Monticello in the sunshine of Indian summer, his white hair ruffled by a warm breeze, facts and thoughts on "Mr. Jefferson" tumbling out in gentle accounts.

"Jefferson was a humanist in the complete sense of the word," said Malone. "Human beings always came first . . . His world is gone. His standards and values went with rural life."

Yet Jefferson's "basic faith in human beings and in the human mind," Malone said, remains the central political theology of America, the legacy of our most talented President. "Jefferson was an excessive optimist," said Malone. "He was an optimist when he probably had no business being an optimist."

"You cannot sum him up. You cannot go back to him for Government programs," said Malone. But in Jefferson is profound thought, curiosity, reason, taste, eloquence and the pursuit of excellence.

By Malone's account on that recent afternoon, Jefferson would have been appalled at the size of Government today, the number of cars on the streets (a prime cause, in Malone's eyes, of urban bad manners), the profit motive in everything, even sports, the ascendancy of merchants and bankers over the more creative farmers and industrialists, the decline of the English language and the idea that you use the White House as a "bully pulpit," in Theodore Roosevelt's phrase.

Today's political campaigning would have shocked him. "He was no man for a crowd," said Malone. "He gave few speeches. His voice was pleasant, but not strong. His career was based on what he wrote."

Jefferson had immense popular appeal. Within the Government, according to Malone, he had "a great gift with people. He exercised leadership over Congress. There was not another President who had such control until Woodrow Wilson."

Jefferson would have been an advocate of many of today's causes, Malone believes. He probably would have been sympathetic to Ralph Nader's consumer crusade and certainly would have been an early member of the Sierra Club, a subscriber to the Save the Whales campaign and most other environmental appeals.

Jefferson, being a gadget man, would have been mesmerized by the White House perquisites—the helicopters, Air Force One. "He would have loved air conditioning, central heating and elevators," declared Malone. "Those things made life more convenient. He would have been fascinated with the modern card catalogue in a library. But I don't know what he would have thought of television." Even in the midst of America's educational marvels, Jefferson probably would have felt pangs of disappointment. "He had a faith in knowledge," said Malone. "He felt that the world would be saved by knowledge. But we have all these libraries groaning with books, and the world has not been saved."

Malone is deep into his sixth volume on Jefferson, and it is a melancholy time for them both. Jefferson is getting old, is beset with debts. He is devastated by inflation and the panic of 1819. His insistence on excellence right up to the end compels him to buy things he cannot afford.

Malone looks ahead despite his failing eyesight. He must have research read to him now, and he must write with the aid of an electronic device. But he still painstakingly turns out a few paragraphs in a day, has finished 21 chapters and thinks there may be another six or eight to go. Like the man he has lived with for much of this century, Malone goes on with grace and "excessive optimism." He is a rare man, another legacy from Thomas Jefferson.

CONCLUDING OBSERVATIONS

The Forums which are reproduced in this volume are in a sense, Mr. Malone's last will and testament to the Miller Center. We could not imagine a more priceless gift nor a nobler heritage. They are now a part of the Center's history.

What others have contributed to his memory represents a gesture at least of thanks for what he meant in our lives and what he did to enrich and inspire our intellectual and moral growth and development. The child of a religious home, he sought to bring those values down to earth. In his scholarly work, to paraphrase the great theologian Paul Tillich, he was one of those who "praised God without ever speaking his name." Dumas' balance in all things, his sense of proportion and discipline, and his consummate politeness provide an example to us all. Yet he thought deeply, felt passionately and researched untiringly on questions that mattered. Because he knew himself, he helped others know Jefferson and the world, beyond any trace of self-pride or pretentiousness of the scholar. Yet in the end, he put his family—Elizabeth, Pam and Gifford—at the center of his life in what he said and did. Those of us who witnessed all this, gained lessons that will outlive even the memory of Malone the biographer and scholar.